Alexander the Great

Coin Portrait of Alexander as Herakles. A silver didrachm showing Alexander with Nemean Lion Helmet, commonly distributed
both during Alexander's reign and afterwards by his Successors.
(Photograph of a coin from the author's collection.)

Winthrop Lindsay Adams

University of Utah

Alexander the Great

Legacy of a Conqueror

New York   San Francisco   Boston
London   Toronto   Sydney   Tokyo   Singapore   Madrid
Mexico City   Munich   Paris   Cape Town   Hong Kong   Montreal

Cover Designer: Laura Shaw
Cover Photo: Detail of Alexander the Great from The Battle of Issus
    Roman Mosaic originally located in the House of the Faun, Pompeii.
    © Araldo de Luca/CORBIS

ISBN 0-321-36582-8

Pro Mea Familia
et
Pro Meis Praeceptoris, Amicis Discipulisque

Totus Unius

Contents

Author's Preface

A group of rebel tribesmen in Afghanistan had fortified a mountainous height called "the Rock," a virtually impregnable position. And so they defied the western commander to take it if he could "find soldiers with wings." The western commander offered rewards and called for volunteers from among his men, and

". . . when all had been assembled who had experience in rock-climbing from previous assaults, there were about 300 in number. They got ready small iron pegs (with which their tents had been secured) to fix into the snow wherever it appeared to be frozen solid or any bare space in the snow which might show through; and they bound the pegs together with strong linen rope. Setting out at night, they went to the most precipitous part of the Rock, because it was the least well guarded. They fixed the pegs into the ground (where it could be seen) or into the snow (where it seemed firmest), each in a different place, and hauled themselves up the Rock. About thirty were killed on the climb, and their bodies were never

> recovered for burial because they fell scattered into the snow below. The rest climbed up around dawn and seized the summit and waved flags to the camp as a signal, following the instructions given them." The western commander then called on the tribesmen to surrender because "he had actually found men with wings, pointing to his soldiers on the heights. . . . The [tribesmen] were astonished at a sight they had never expected, and assumed the soldiers occupying the Rock were both more numerous and fully armed; they surrendered." (Arrian, 4.19.1-4)

This incident could have happened last year, but in fact the western commander was Alexander the Great, the 300 troops were his Macedonians assaulting the legendary Rock of Sogdiana in what is now probably northeastern Afghanistan, and the time was more than 2300 years ago. This is as good an introduction as any to what is fascinating about the story of Alexander the Great: It is both as fresh as yesterday and more than two millennia old. Alexander has always embodied dichotomies to both his contemporaries and those who have come after him. Some who knew him, among both the Macedonians and those he conquered, literally thought he was a god; others who knew him, even among the Macedonians, hated and feared him as a tyrant.

Much of this incongruity has to do with what he achieved in his lifetime. The conquest of the

Persian Empire, which was roughly the size of the United States of America and had a population of about eighty million people, was itself a greater-than-life-size achievement. He accomplished this in a little more than ten years with an army that was never more than 50,000 men, fighting on foot and horseback. The seemingly insurmountable odds, limited resources, and sheer audacity of the venture have created a romanticized picture of Alexander, even among his opponents. And this mythic image was just as present during his lifetime as it is now.

It is hardly surprising today that Alexander is viewed as the very symbol of ancient Greek culture, but most Greeks at the time would have scoffed at this idea. Both during his time and since, he has been seen as the agent spreading Greek culture and civilization to the East. He also sowed terror and destruction. Though a symbol of Western civilization, he got into the most trouble with his own countrymen for adopting Eastern customs and trying to bridge the cultural gap between East and West. He has been romanticized as a civilizer in an area that had, in fact, been civilized far longer than Greece. Though he created an empire that stretched from the Adriatic to modern Pakistan, it was one that did not outlast him. Indeed, the effect of his actions was to break up an area, the Persian Empire, whose unity had lasted for more than two centuries. Alexander has been presented as a brilliant commander and a military genius, but equally as a moody and volatile character who often failed to grasp strategic realities and hated details. He was noted as a generous and loyal friend, but he also could be ruthless to friend and foe alike. For instance, he ran one of his best friends through with a pike at a drunken feast and killed others on trumped-up charges at show trials.

These contrasts in Alexander's character and achievements were well known in antiquity. His myth grew while he was still alive, and it makes distinguishing the historical Alexander from the apocryphal ones all the harder. Alexander is illusory, and yet we have more written material on him than any other figure from Classical Antiquity. Five major sources on Alexander have survived from the ancient period, but the earliest one was written almost three centuries after his death and the best one was written 200 years after that. And those are just the more substantial histories. Alexander's contemporaries, much as those who campaigned with Napoleon or fought in World War II, left books and journals of their adventures and struggles. Official journals, day books, and geographic descriptions were ordered kept by Alexander and survived him. But they have come down to us only in fragments.

There are countless tales and stories about Alexander and his exploits. In the century after his death, a popular work of fiction, *The Alexander Romance*, introduced in historical garb outright fabrications, such as a correspondence between Alexander and Darius, filled with outlandish statements and events. For all intents and purposes, it was the first historical novel and was wildly popular. There are more than eighty Greek versions of these stories alone, as well as even more fanciful versions in Egyptian (Coptic), Armenian, Syriac, and Arabic. Beyond this, Alexander in one form or another shows up in folk traditions ranging from Icelandic sagas to Malaysian royal genealogies. He appears in Jewish tradition as, among other things, the one who shuts Gog and Magog behind the Iron Gate of Debend and thus preserves the world. In the *Koran*, he is Dhul-Qarnein, the Horned One, from the rams-horn portrait which was most common on his coins, along with his faithful adviser, Aristu (Aristotle). The Arabic form of his name, Iskander, follows him throughout the Islamic world. His imagined descendants crowd both sides of the Khyber Pass.

In the Western context, Alexander's tradition is equally long, but no less fanciful in its way. On seeing a portrait bust of Alexander in Spain, Caesar wept thinking about what Alexander had accomplished, while he had yet to achieve greatness. Alexander became an exemplar of the conquering hero for Augustus and Trajan. Napoleon had his officers read Arrian's account of Alexander on his own eighteenth-century expedition to Egypt, the ultimate goal of which was to dislodge the British from India. After all, Alexander had reached India via Egypt. The British took Napoleon's threat to India seriously for the very same reason. But the dichotomy of Alexander's character and reputation is equally apparent. He was imitated by such questionable figures as the Emperor Caligula, and was so slavishly copied by the Emperor Caracalla that the emperor not only dressed himself as Alexander and nicknamed his generals after Alexander's commanders, but formed a Macedonian phalanx within the Roman army more than 500 years after Alexander's death. That would be roughly the same as sending a historical group recreating a unit from the American Revolutionary War into Desert Storm. In the Medieval Christian tradition, Alexander was a favorite topic for sermons and homilies. He was used as an example of the good and virtuous king, of the good king gone bad, and of the bad king gone worse. He was all these things at one time or another.

Alexander was a complex character and is no less so to the modern era. Since serious historical study of Classical Antiquity began in the nineteenth century, Alexander has been a central figure. He has the largest bibliography of any figure from ancient history except Christ. Each generation, asking its own questions, remakes him. To some, such as Sir William Woodthorpe Tarn, he was a far-thinking idealistic hero trying to change the world for the good. To others, such as Ernst Badian or A. B. Bosworth, he was a ruthless dictator carrying out ethnic cleansing. To those in between, he was seen as a loyal friend, a hated enemy, a drunkard, an actor, a megalomaniac, a lover, a lost soul, and a brilliant soldier. This book will not answer the question, "Which one of these was he?" Indeed, he may have been all of them at once. But it will introduce the topics, the contexts, the character, and the achievements of a figure who clearly touched the world in a way no one has since.

Lastly, this biography of Alexander the Great is part of a series, Longman's Weekend Biography series, which is designed to discuss significant figures who have been actors on the world stage, but have also been acted upon by the world. From the very beginning Alexander deliberately sought such a platform for his achievements, first for the Greek world, then the Near East and Asia. It was an arena that grew as his journey continued, with repercussions that went far beyond anything he could possibly have imagined. But one should note as the narrative unfolds that the world had an impact on Alexander as well. One can see it in his drive to find the limits of the world in the Danube, the Nile, the Indus or the "Ocean," but also in the impact that the societies he encountered had on how he would define himself and his empire.

Acknowledgments

I have approached this project as if it were a kind of extended and informed conversation about Alexander. In doing so, it strikes me that it is the sum of over three decades of conversations I have had about Alexander with my teachers, my colleagues, and my students. In his frequently underrated *History of Rome*, Velleius Patercullus stated that despite his haste, Caesar "placed his hand on my pen and forced me to stay a while with him." So it was with Alexander for me. My first graduate seminar at Virginia was on "Alexander and the Hellenistic World" and the first specialty class I taught as a professor at Utah likewise was on Alexander. I would like now to acknowledge those people who got me involved in this and have sustained that conversation for so long.

First of all of these is the late Harry Dell, my mentor, who taught that seminar (and me) about not just Alexander, but about Philip, Macedonia, and Greece, as well as how to be a teacher. He was taken too soon and is still much missed by family, friends, colleagues, and students alike. Equally important is Gene Borza, the dean of Macedonian Studies in this country, whose knowledge of Macedonia is reflected throughout this book and who is in all things the very model of a professional and a friend.

The late N.G.L. Hammond inspired several generations of Macedonian scholars and was invariably personable and generous to young scholars (such as I then was). Peter Green is always the perfect example of good writing and excellent scholarship; as with Gene Borza, the ideas and examples of Hammond and Green greatly influenced this book. So too did Ernst Badian, who has written on Alexander for over half a century, always employing an exhaustive scholarship that combines keen insight and far-ranging ideas. The ideas on frontiers, Macedonian, Asian, or otherwise, owe a great deal to John Eadie, my favorite Roman historian. The relationship between Macedonia and the Greeks in the fourth century has been both informed and kept on track by many discussions with Charles Hamilton and Jim Chambers. Finally, one must mention the late Charles Farrell Edson, who is the intellectual father of Ancient Macedonian

Studies in this country. He trained Harry Dell, and through him me as well. His work, especially on early Macedonia, is evident throughout.

Among the liveliest discussions I have enjoyed on Alexander were the ones with fellow students of Harry Dell at Virginia. Ed Anson and I were in seminars together, and oddly always seemed to choose the opposite sides of issues and controversies. The result was that we sharpened each other's arguments, learned a great deal, and maintained a friendship now almost thirty-five years old. We were soon joined by Frank Collins, a friend since my first year in college, who managed to keep the conversation amongst us honest. He has served his country abroad for over 20 years, but academe lost a great scholar and teacher. Bill Greenwalt and Frank Holt were students who came after us, Harry's last, and in many ways, best students. Most of the ideas on the early Argeads in this book come from the work of Bill Greenwalt, and we have faithfully read many of each other's manuscripts for decades. Frank Holt is the leading scholar working on Alexander and the East, as well as the Greeks in Asia. Much of the picture of those topics in this endeavor benefits from his work.

There is a host of scholars whose work has directly informed me and the study of Alexander. Among them are friends such as: Waldemar

Heckel, Canada's leading scholar on Alexander and the sources for him; Elizabeth Carney, who has done so much to open up gender studies in Macedonian history; Joseph Roisman, who has done more to put Alexander studies in context than anyone I know, for both students and colleagues; Jack Ellis, whose work on Philip and Macedonia has always been fruitful and original; and Carol Thomas, whose interest in Greek kingship in any age is always insightful and informative. All of these scholars have aided in my journey; any errors are mine alone.

Acknowledgements are also given to the reviewers who helped shape this work: Mark E. Gunn, Meridian Community College; Rhett Leverett, Marymount University; and William Morison, Grand Valley State University. Finally, I could not have done this without the help of the excellent editorial and production staff at Longman Publishers.

I hope this work will help introduce new students to this ancient conversation on Alexander the Great and that Alexander will "place his hand on their pens and force them to stay awhile." If they do so, they will find those studies filled with rich material, interesting questions, and many good friends with whom to share them.

WINTHROP LINDSAY ADAMS

Alexander the Great

Prologue

The Macedonian Background

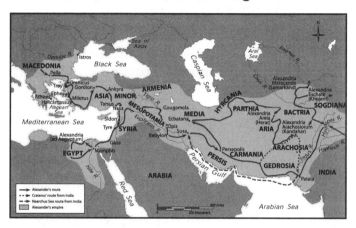

Alexander's Empire

Introduction

As with all people, Alexander the Great was a product of the family and society into which he was born and the place in which he grew up. The perspectives by which he viewed the world, and indeed his remarkable appreciation for the diversity of the cultures through which he passed, as well as the cross-cultural exchange that took place between them, are largely attributable to those factors. For Alexander was more than a conqueror, and the appeal of his personality went beyond his own culture to make him a world figure. He was sometimes loved and sometimes hated, both within his own society, and more remarkably, by the world at large. Alexander saw himself as a figure on that world stage, as did both those who knew him and those who came after him. But before we look at Alexander and that world, it is important to understand from where he came and what shaped his views.

Macedon: The Land

On a number of levels, Macedonia occupied a unique place in Greek history and the Greek landscape. It possessed no geographic unity, which would naturally bind the area together. More important is the fact that Macedonia lay on both the major east-west and north-south communications routes in the Balkans. Later on the Romans would build a road to capitalize on the East-West routes: the Via Egnatia. For a strong state, this road would put it in the perfect position to exploit these areas for expansion, especially to the east and south. A weak state, however, would be open to invasion virtually from all directions. Which of these fates was to predominate in Macedonia depended on the strength or craftiness of the monarch himself, down to the reign of Philip II, Alexander's father.

At Macedonia's heart was the largest plains area in Greece, which lay along the western shores of the Thermaic Gulf. The plain was watered by two great, deep-flowing rivers. As a consequence, Macedonia was not only the largest plains area in Greece, but the most fertile. The rich crops made the area a prime target for the wilder upland tribal peoples who came from less fertile areas of the Balkans.

Beyond this plain, Macedonia was ringed by mountains, falling out in semicircles like onionskins all the way to the Adriatic Sea. These barriers were pierced at several points by highland cull passes (broad gorges), which made the area perfectly suited not only for moving sheep and goats from lowland winter pasturage to highland summer herdsteads, but also for moving people.

The highlands opened up into broad, upland valleys, filled with lakes and plains. They were as rich agriculturally as they were isolated geographically. These areas supported large populations that were politically independent and self-reliant principalities down to the reign of Philip II, Alexander's father. The political assimilation of these highland groups would constitute the chief internal problem for the Argead dynasty of Macedon, Alexander's family.

The mountains were heavily forested, and timber was one of the Argeads' chief exports, as these were the best shipbuilding timbers in the Mediterranean. Natural resources, in addition to the forests and land, included deposits of gold and silver. The area abounded in game: wild boar, wild cattle, deer, aurochs, and lions. Hunting was, indeed, the chief Macedonian passion. The land yielded all types of cereal crops in both the broad valleys and the plains. Also, the orchards and vineyards of Macedonia were legendary in antiquity, and its vineyards are still the source of the best wines in Greece today.

Wild roses sprang up naturally in the region, especially where the mountains dropped off to the Emathian plain. Framed by waterfalls, it was an area of spectacular beauty, known in antiquity as the Gardens of Midas. The plains areas also supported large herds of cattle and horses, providing Macedonia's first military asset because horses were fed the same grains that people ate in the ancient world (wheat, barley, and spelt, rather than the oats on which they thrive today). The more grain the horses were fed, the larger they could be bred and the greater the number that could be supported. As the largest plains area in Greece, Macedonia produced a surplus in grain which could be used to develop their horse-breeding stock to standards comparable in size to modern horses. Macedonian horses, along with those of Thessaly, Macedonia's neighboring district just south of Mount Olympus, were the best in Greece—and consequently they produced the best cavalry mounts as well.

The People

The people who occupied this land were an equally distinct lot. Their foundation legends stated that they were descended from a son of Zeus, Makedon, who in turn had two sons, Pieros and Amathos (these provided a religious history to already existing geographic and ethnic terms). They spoke a dialect called Makednic, vaguely related to Aeolic or to northwest Greek, but distinct enough to be practically unintelligible to the Ionic- and Doric-speaking Greeks to the south. The Macedonian highlanders had a tough life, physically from their environment and politically from their neighbors, and tended to see themselves as distinct from their Greek cousins. The nature of the land produced serious, self-reliant individuals who loved life because it was uncertain. They drank heavily, lived hard, fought often, and usually died both violently and young.

Beyond the Macedonians in the west and northwest were the Illyrians. These were groups speaking languages close to (but not) Greek. Their basic organization was tribal, and their

high mountain valleys kept them even more isolated than were the Macedonians. The land was
much poorer than Macedonia, however, and the
Illyrians suffered from frequent crop shortages
and subsequent overpopulation. This forced the
Illyrians to raid the more settled Macedonian
lands to the east and south in order to survive. A
constant raiding culture emerged, which on occasion would snowball into a major invasion under a successful Illyrian chieftain, as other tribes
would throw in with the victorious chief and
even proclaim him "King" of Illyria. The result
was that the Macedonian upland valley chiefdoms were subject to constant raids and frequent invasions from the Illyrians. As these areas
came under the domination of the Argead dynasty, this became its problem as well.

Virtually identical conditions existed directly
to the north of the Macedonians. The Paeonians
and Pelagonians, tribal peoples of undetermined
ethnic origin, kept constant pressure on Macedon.
To the northeast and east of Macedonia, the
chief problem came from the Thracians, another
major group made up of a much larger collection
of tribes and a larger overall population. Indeed,
the whole eastern side of the Pindus and what
later became the Argead Macedonian heartland
were originally occupied by two Thracian tribes:
the Pieres and the Bottiaoi. These had been driven

out or absorbed when Pieria and the Emathian plain were occupied by the Argead Macedonians, which brought the monarchy in contact with other Thracian tribes such as the Sithones, Edones, and Odryssai.

The result was that the Makednic peoples were bordered on the west, north, and east by a ring of hostile tribes that were a constant military threat to Macedonia's very existence. This constituted one of two major external problems for the Macedonians (the other being their civilized Greek cousins to the south, who completed the ring, and who will be addressed later). Macedonia was, in effect, a buffer for the southern Greeks for most of its independent history, a shield against barbarian invasion which failed only once during its entire history, when a brief incursion by Celtic tribal raiders in 279 B.C.E. swept all the way into central Greece.

But this also meant that Macedonia was a frontier zone, not unlike the popular image of the American West, where those who slept far from their weapons were not long to remain in this world. The difference was that, while the picture of the American frontier was largely the creation of a lurid eastern United States press, in ancient Macedonia it was all too real. Even after Macedonia had become a Roman province, one of its governors in the first century B.C.E., Quintus

Tullius Cicero, wrote to his brother, the great orator Marcus Tullius Cicero, that it was an area "which so many barbarian nations adjoin that for its governors, the boundaries are identical with the points of their own swords and spears" (*In Pisonem*, 16.38). This frontier state was an overriding fact of life for the Macedonians, one that was reflected in both their political and social institutions.

Political Organization

Largely because of the necessity for quick action in the event of barbarian raids, the institution of kingship remained the common form of government in the north; whereas in southern Greece, with the exception of Sparta, it had been replaced by aristocracy, oligarchy, or democracy, depending on time and place. Kingship was common to most peoples in their early stages of development. It was especially useful in the periods of the great migrations and as such can be found among Celtic-, Germanic-, Iranian-, and Italic-speaking peoples as well as the Greeks. Because it is first characterized in Western literature in the *Iliad* and the *Odyssey*, this early political organization is frequently called a "Homeric war monarchy."

In Macedonia, each mountain valley and tribal area had its own king or chieftain, and these remained virtually independent down to the fifth century B.C.E. Even after that, depending on the strength of the individual Argead monarch, these areas were semi-independent down to the time of Philip and Alexander. Each area was self-supporting agriculturally because of good land and pasturage, and self-supporting politically and militarily because it had to be. These largely autonomous areas formed the upland cantons of the Argead monarchy under Philip II, who sought to integrate them into a Macedonian state. He saw them as districts, whereas before they had seen themselves as separate entities.

The political and social institutions characteristic of these tribes can be found among many other early groups, or for that matter most nomadic groups. A free warrior assembly was comprised of all free adult males capable of bearing arms and usually was simply called by the tribal name. In Macedonia's case this was *hoi Makedonoi* (the Macedonians). They elected a *basileus* (king or chief) from among the male members of a princely house and fought under his command as a tribal militia. Normally, this chieftain would have a Council of Elders made up of the heads of the important families, whose role was to advise the *basileus*. A term (*Pelagones*) for such an institution existed in Macedonia, but by the end of the sixth century B.C.E. there is no active trace of the institution itself. Though the king usually had a group of friends to advise him, it was not a formal body as in the other Greek states. Among those southern Greek states it was kingship that faded away or was absorbed by the Council of Elders. In the north, because of the frontier conditions and the need for a strong executive to make quick decisions, it was the Council of Elders that disappeared and kingship that remained.

The king was first and foremost the military commander of his people. If he failed to perform in this area, historic example shows that he was removed, either naturally or otherwise. He was also the chief priest and chief judge. Until the time of Philip and Alexander, the upland tribes maintained a fierce loyalty to these princely houses, which prevented the total unification of Macedonia until Philip's state building program in the fourth century.

One last political and social institution needs attention. The king maintained a band of hand-picked mounted warriors, which formed the fighting elite. These were called the Hetairoi, or Companions of the king. They were a highly mobile strike force intended to counter raids and a pool from which to draw officers and commanders for the tribal militia infantry. These men were, in some cases, relatives of the king, but mostly they were the sons of the chief families of the realm. They were supported by grants of land and gifts from the king and were the basis for the Macedonian army, whose cavalry was famed from the earliest times.

Social and Religious Customs

Customs among the Macedonians were equally distinct, mirroring in some ways other Greek societies, but always reflecting both unique ethnic Macedonian variations and the customs of those different ethnic groups absorbed by the Macedonians. Also, they show the influence of Macedonia being a frontier society. Most importantly, this experience with different religious and social customs helped shape Alexander's attitude toward incorporating the societies he encountered in the East.

The best way to see this is to look at some of these customs. The first group reflected holdovers from a more primitive time. Aristotle states, for instance, that in the early days of the kingdom, a Macedonian who had not yet killed an enemy in hand-to-hand combat had to wear a sash around his waist, demonstrative of a rite of passage. There is clear evidence of blood feuds even down to Philip's day, a trait held in common with early Greek society but which had passed out of Greek custom several centuries before. The Alexandrian Greek writer Athenaeus states that anyone in

Macedonia who had not killed a wild boar without the use of a net had to sit in a chair at banquets (rather than reclining): another rite of passage. It is a telling point here that Athenaeus relates this in discussing the fact that Cassander, king of Macedonia after Alexander, had to sit this way, for he had never accomplished the feat. The king was not above social custom, let alone the law. The favorite social pastimes were feasting, drinking (symposia), and hunting, all of which were done prodigiously. The end of a banquet (not the beginning) was always announced by a trumpet call, probably because of the number of times feasting had been ended by a genuine call to arms to fend off a barbarian raid.

The second group was made up of more formal customs. Among the chief national religious festivals were ritual dances such as the *Telesias*, a dance of armed warriors, and the *Karpeia*, which celebrated cattle rustling—a warrior ritually stole oxen from a herder. One of the marriage ceremony customs involved cutting a loaf of bread with a sword held by the bride and groom together. Army purification rites took place in the spring and autumn, the opening and closing of the campaigning season. This was a custom designed to prepare individuals psychologically for combat, as well as to deal with the post-traumatic aspects of fighting. It involved the sacrifice of a hunting dog, with the army marching between the two halves of the dog and then engaging in a mock combat. In the autumn, this would also involve elaborate funeral rites for the fallen, presided over by the king, and with single combats (*monomachia*) between picked warriors. This last clearly demonstrates the Homeric nature of the society, a version of the funeral rites for Patroklos in the *Iliad*.

Specific religious cults included the festival of the Hetairideia, in honor of Zeus Hetairides, which celebrated the sacred relationship which bound the king and his companions together. The cult of Heracles Kynagidas (the Huntsman) honored the *basilokoi kynegoi*, the royal hunting dog handlers, and hunting as an institution. There were, indeed, a large number of cults, in all of which the king was involved as the chief celebrant. One of these was personal to the royal house: Heracles Propator (the Forefather), who was the titular founder of the Argead house.

Others, equally celebrated and official, were derived from the Thracian groups that had been absorbed by the Macedonians during the monarchy's expansion further onto the plains. In particular there was the cult of Sabazius, the wilder Thracian version of Dionysus, which Euripides portrayed in his play *The Bacchae*, a play written at the Macedonian court. This involved much drinking and frenzied dancing, along with the furious women's rites of the Klodones and Mimallonai, and satyr worship, the Sauadai. Gazoria, the Thracian version of the Greek Goddess of the Hunt, Artemis, was equally important, as was Zeirene, the Thracian Aphrodite. One would presume that Illyrian customs to the west and Paeonian ones to the north were incorporated as well, though they would be hard to separate from the general practice.

Nothing could demonstrate the culturally diverse nature of the Macedonians better. In fact, there were two meanings to the term "Macedonian." The one with which we have been dealing is the ethnic term, but there was also a political definition. To be a Macedonian in this sense meant to hold land from the king in exchange for military service, and all land was technically king's land, so all landholders were citizens. This status was the king's to confer, both on ethnic Macedonians and others: Greeks, Thracians, Illyrians, Paeonians, or whomever. Holding land in this sense amounted to the Macedonian definition of citizenship, and the important factor here is that it was not ethnically restrictive. The right was often extended to include other ethnic groups, thereby providing for the genuine incorporation of different elements into Macedonian society rather than simply their subjugation or conquest. This point will be essential to understanding Alexander's approach to empire and the peoples who came under his rule.

The Argead Monarchy

The fate of the north might have been very different. The interior highlands might have remained split into a half dozen upland regions and never united. The reason that it did not was the development of the Argead monarchy, which would unite first the lowland area around the plains and Thermaic Gulf and then move into the highlands.

There is only a handful of references dealing with early Macedonian history: a few sentences in Hesiod, Herodotus, Thucydides, Diodorus of Sicily, and some fragments of the Athenian tragedian Euripides' play the *Archelaus*, which celebrated the founding of the Argead dynasty. Somewhere around 700 B.C.E., a highland clan, which claimed descent from Herakles and the royal Temenid house of Argos in southern Greece, migrated from Orestis, down the Haliacmon River and into Pieria, where they founded a kingdom at the foot of Mount Olympus.

A pronouncement from the Delphic Oracle of Apollo told one of the later chiefs to settle further into Bottiaia, on the plains, and to establish a city where he found goats grazing. The city was Aegae, "Goat Place," which became the Argead capital. From there, they spread out to the west and north, occupying first the foothills and then moving out onto the plains. This included seizing the Thracian stronghold at Edessa, which controlled the main road west.

This expansion was against the Thracian tribes of the area, which were overwhelmed and absorbed, in the case of the Pieres, and which partially absorbed and partially drove out the Bottiaoi. These two districts formed the heartland of the kingdom. Expansion also brought the Argeads up against Illyrian raiders for the first time. The Argead kings had the same political customs and institutions as the other Makednic groups. The king was military commander, judge, and chief priest of his people. The office was elective within the royal family.

An intensely personal relationship existed between king and people. It was the Macedonian right to have the king not simply command but actually to lead the army, and from the front rank. This was taken most seriously. However, the nature of the relationship was conditional, and the king's powers were not absolute. As a judge, he was required to hear petitions from his people, even under circumstances with which he would rather not have to deal. One of Alexander's successors, Demetrius Poliorcetes, the "Sacker of

Cities," was berated for not attending to his du
ties and ultimately abandoned as king. This right
of petition, or isegoria (free speech, for all intents
and purposes), was a hallmark of Macedonian
tradition. Equally, the king could not execute anyone out of hand for treason, but rather brought
the accused to trial before the Macedonians, the
army assembly. The king acted in the role of
prosecutor, but the army was the judge, jury, and
executioner. If found guilty, the accused was
stoned to death by the assembly. A popular and
strong king might literally get away with a murder, but it was rare, and even so powerful a figure
as Alexander tended to use the legal approach.

The political definition of "Macedonian"
(holding land from the king in exchange for military service) has already been mentioned. That
meant that citizenship itself was based on personal service rather than blood relationship. It
denotes a contractual arrangement between the
king and a free people. One can see this in the
way the kings were raised and what was expected
of them. Kings were to lead their people in all
things, as first among equals. The sons of the
ruling house were trained with the royal pages
(basilokoi paides), that is, the sons of Companions and chief families of the state. These young
warriors were raised almost like a pack of hunting dogs, serving as squires and attendants,

learning discipline and how to take orders, before they were expected to give and enforce them. The other royal pages would be the Companions of the next generation. In doing so they learned the profession of arms, how to hunt and kill, as well as to other Macedonian passions like drinking and feasting.

In all of this, the Macedonian king was expected to excel, for the Macedonians were a rough lot, and he had to be the roughest of the lot. He was expected to be the hardest drinker, finest horseman, and most adept hunter of the group, as well as to demonstrate the greatest prowess in arms. He had to lead his people in all things. The general picture we get is of the typical Homeric war monarchy, a society rather reflective of Achilles and Agamemnon.

The Growth of the Argead Monarchy

Oddly, the first glimmer of a truly historical Macedonia comes from its contact with Persia, just as that will be Alexander's platform to the world stage. That light was thrown off by Darius the Great and his Scythian expedition of about 512 B.C.E. In order to protect his left flank as he moved the Persian Grand Army to the Danube River, Darius sent forces to subdue the powerful Thracian tribes of the Bisaltai, Odomanti, and Edonians who occupied the territory up to the

Strymon River. This move put the Persians on the borders of Macedonia.

Emissaries were sent to the court of Amyntas I, the Argead king of Macedonia, asking for the traditional signs of symbolic submission to the Persian Great King: earth and water. These were given, and a marriage alliance sealed the relationship. Macedonia became a Persian vassal state.

This did not prevent all independent action, and it was Alexander I Philhellenos, the son and successor to Amyntas, who supplied Athens with the ship timber for the fleet which would later defeat the Persians at Salamis and save Greece. As such, Alexander I was named not only *Proxenos* (spokesman) for Athens, but also "Benefactor of the Athenian People." Nevertheless, he was forced to participate in Xerxes' invasion of Greece. There was virtually no chance Alexander I could stand against Xerxes and his Persian Grand Army, which amounted to some 180,000 men, but he did warn the Greek allied forces not to make a stand at the Vale of Tempe (probably by telling them that it could be turned inland in no fewer than four places and was therefore a deathtrap).

Alexander I and the Macedonian cavalry were pressed into Persian service both because of the excellence of the cavalry and, one suspects, as hostages for the good behavior of the kingdom.

Following the Persian naval defeat at Salamis, Xerxes tried to secure Alexander's loyalty by increasing the size of the Argead kingdom to include the upland principalities. Though Alexander I accepted authority over these regions, as a bribe it didn't work. At the Battle of Plataea in 479 B.C.E., where the Greek allied army routed the Persians, an unknown horseman warned the Greeks of the Persian intentions and made the victory possible. Afterward, Alexander I let it be known that he was that horseman. Whether it was true or a propaganda ploy to increase his prestige, Alexander did change sides and now turned on the remnants of the Persian forces. At the main crossing of the Strymon River, on the borders of his kingdom, Alexander I fell on the Persians. What ensued was a complete disaster, and few Persians made it back. With the spoils of the victory, Alexander dedicated a gold statue at the Oracle of Apollo at Delphi to commemorate his role in the Greek victory.

Even more important, as the Persian presence in the north collapsed, it left behind a power vacuum and a golden opportunity for the expansion of the Argead orbit. The easternmost point of this expansion was on the Strymon, and Alexander assumed the control of the Thracian tribe of the Bisaltai as well as the rich hinterlands behind the Chalcidic peninsula, the Anthemous. The new areas held gold and silver mines and increased royal revenues by more than 350 silver talents a year. A talent was a specific unit of weight (about 26 kilograms), but its purchase power was far greater in antiquity; the annual income for the Athenian empire at its height in the fifth century, when it controlled the entire Aegean Sea basin, was about 1200 silver talents. The new lands were parcelled out, increasing the number of Companions and also, by definition, the number of Macedonians. Alexander I now began to mint coins in his own name.

Alexander had quadrupled the size of his kingdom and now began to incorporate the new areas into a greater Macedonia. He organized formal cavalry squadrons (other than the Companions) for both the highlands and Macedonian heartland. At this point the army assembly was probably also offically recognized as an institution, and intended to be used as a counterbalance to the upland princes.

But expansion brought new problems. These highland chiefdoms constituted a considerable internal threat to Argead authority. The highland areas tried to maintain their autonomy against Argeads. They saw the authority of Alexander I as no more than titular at best, and from now down to the time of Philip II these cantons would alternately try to break away or interfere and actually take over the government. Frequently these princes would cooperate with outside groups to achieve their ends. Illyrians, Paeonians, Thracians, and Athens, which sought to expand its control in the north, all sought to use them to destroy the central government and thereby open Argead Macedonia to exploitation.

The external threats were equally persistent and twofold. First, there were the traditional barbarian incursions from the Illyrians, Paeonians, and Thracians. The second was the intrusion into the area by the Macedonians' civilized cousins to the south. In the fifth century, this increasingly brought them into conflict with Athens and its growing empire. Athens coveted both the silver and gold resources around Mount Pangeion and Macedonia's control of the timber trade, which was vital for the Athenian fleet. So the kingdom was pressured from all sides.

Fifth-Century Macedonia

The territorial expansion of Macedonia brought a new menace which threatened the kingdom for the next three generations: the growing control of the northern Aegean basin, and especially the Greek towns along the coasts, by Athens. Macedonia was transformed in Athens' eyes from an ally into a rival for the domination of this area. Athens was increasingly unwilling to depend on Macedonian good will. The result was an inevitable confrontation between the two powers, which had previously been friends and allies.

While Alexander I Philhellenos lived, Athens could accomplish little in this area, but Alexander I died around 450 B.C.E. He had achieved a great deal in his long reign. He had united, in name at least, all the Macedonians and created a state with the largest land area in Greece. He had brought Macedonia fully into the Greek orbit. From this point on, the destinies of Macedonia and Greece would be tied together, although they did not know this at the time.

Alexander was succeeded by his son, Perdikkas II. His immediate relations with Athens are unknown, though Athens would later view him as a symbol of craftiness and treachery. Treaties technically died with the king who negotiated them, so Perdikkas may not have inherited his father's relationship with Athens.

When Thucydides opens his narrative of the Peloponnesian War, Athens is already at war with Perdikkas in 436 B.C.E., four years before Athens goes to war against Sparta. Specifically, Athens is backing a rival claimant to the throne. At the same time, they try again and succeed in establishing a colony at the Strymon River, a new city called Amphipolis which was a panhellenic foundation (its population drawn from throughout the allied states, not just Athens) which will later give the city independent ambitions. Two years later, Athens took the city of Methone on the Macedonian coast and brought it into the Delian League. They also stirred the upland princely houses against Perdikkas. Athens seized the town of Therme at the head of the Thermaic Gulf, the site of the modern Thessaloniki.

Down to his death, around 412 B.C.E., Perdikkas was caught between Athens and Sparta in the titanic struggle for the domination of Greece. Just to keep his kingdom together in the face of incursions directly by Athens, or by its agents among the Thracians, Illyrians, and rebellious upcountry princes, was an achievement. Perdikkas was continually switching from one side to the other, and alternately declaring his neutrality, to try to keep things together. It was this vacillation that gained him the reputation among the Athenians for double dealing and betrayal, but when one realizes his point of view and that loyalty to the Macedonian kingdom was his only duty, he becomes more sympathetic.

His successor was his son, Archelaus, who was able to take advantage of the renewed struggle between Athens and Sparta to establish firmly Macedonia's neutral status. Both sides in the Peloponnesian War had considerably weakened themselves in the struggle, and both needed

Macedonian cooperation for naval stores, Archelaus happily sold to both sides. In an attempt to secure his favor, the Athenians even granted Archelaus the same status that Alexander I had held as Proxenos and Benefactor of the Athenian People.

Freedom from Athenian pressure gave Archelaus the time to consolidate his position and develop the kingdom. He began to build a network of roads to tie the kingdom together, along with a string of fortresses to protect upper Macedonia from barbarian raids. In doing so he strengthened royal authority and the central government. Some of the intrigues of the highland princes ranged from trying to break away from the Argead kingdom to attempts at controlling the whole kingdom from within.

The army was put on a more regular footing, according to Thucydides, with regular sources of horses, weapons, and supplies. Tribal militia were organized into infantry units equipped as hoplites, heavy-armed warriors typical of the kind used by the Greek city-states. Cavalry squadrons from all the cantons were likewise reorganized. Thucydides states that Archelaus did more than all his predecessors in this regard.

In 410 B.C.E., to secure the kingdom's position and insulate it from Athenian and Spartan influence, Archelaus seized the town of Pydna, on the coast east of Mount Olympos, as a counterpoint to the Athenian-held city of Methone. He also put a pro-Macedonian party in control of Larissa in northern Thessaly, and thus protected both the major passes into the kingdom from the south.

Archelaus moved the administrative capital of the kingdom from Aegae, in the foothills of Mount Olympos, to Pella, a port city located on the Loudias River and which opened onto the Thermaic Gulf. This made communications with the Aegean and with the Greek states easier. Aegae remained as a religious capital and summer palace. Archelaus fostered trade by changing to the Persian standard of coinage. To increase manufacturing, he brought all kinds of artisans into Pella from throughout Greece. With war raging elsewhere in the Aegean, Pella became a refuge from the strife and grew into a bustling city.

This all had a profound effect on the Macedonian court. Attic Greek, the dialect of Greek spoken in Athens, now became the official court and governmental language. All laws and decrees were published in it; all public business was conducted in it. Commercial, civil, and criminal laws were modelled after Athens' laws, so that Athens, which normally established treaty rights for its citizens in foreign countries, did not need to protect its citizens who had business in

Macedon. Greeks had been settling in Macedonia since Alexander I's time, but this immigration now increased, along with a steady process of hellenization.

The Macedonian court had always patronized poets. To Archelaus' court came the most gifted artists of the day: painters like Zeuxis of Heraclea, who decorated the royal palace; the epic poet Choerilius; the choral poet Timarchus; and the tragedian Agathon of Athens (later made famous in Plato's *Symposium*). But the most famous and successful of this group of emigrés was the tragic playwright Euripides, who left Athens after the production of the *Trojan Women*. He had used this play as a vehicle for criticizing Athenian imperialistic actions, resulting in his being fined a huge sum. Euripides became a Hetairos at Archelaus' court and wrote at least two plays there. The first was the *Bacchae,* which reflects the wilder Macedonian version of Dionysus worship, and the other was the *Archelaus*, which celebrated the founding of the Macedonian royal house. Honored and made a Macedonian, Euripides later died there as the result of a hunting accident. The Macedonians thought of him as their own, and he was buried in the royal cemetery at Aegae.

Archelaus virtually transformed Macedonia into one of the great powers of the Aegean. The kingdom was cultured and rose in repute throughout the Greek world. But though it achieved external stability, the problem of central authority versus the fractious highland chiefdoms re-emerged. Archelaus was assassinated in 399 B.C.E. by a disgruntled noble, which began a new period of anarchy in Macedonia that almost brought the kingdom down.

The Period of Anarchy

Once the way was reopened for court intrigue following Archelaus' assassination, it seemed impossible to stop. His son, Orestes, was too young to succeed directly to the throne, so a regency was set up under his uncle, Aeropus, who promptly killed the boy and became Aeropus II. In a brief flurry of killings and deaths over a period of five years, Macedonia saw five kings die, and the direct line of Perdikkas II was wiped out. The rule passed to a cousin, Amyntas III.

Amyntas III was descended from the younger son of Alexander the Philhellene. Despite the legacy of bloodshed which brought him to the throne, Amyntas was to rule for some 24 years and, against all odds, died a natural death in 370 B.C.E. But the intervening years were eventful. His position was shaky and he could keep himself in power only by playing the more powerful elements, both within and outside his kingdom, off against one another. He managed this, for the most part, by paying tribute to northern barbarians, and by trading away Macedonian lands to Greek powers such as Athens, Thebes, and Thessaly. There was also a new group, the emerging Chalcidic League, made up of some 20 Greek cities on the Chalcidic peninsula, just east of Macedonia and below the rich Anthemous region acquired by Alexander I.

Amyntas was driven out by the Chalcidic League (Koinon) and its chief town, Olynthus, in 385 B.C.E., and a pretender was put on the throne. Amyntas, however, was nothing if not resilient. He enlisted help from one of the upland princes and from the Spartans, who put him back on the throne in 382 B.C.E. The 370s B.C.E. saw the resurgence of Athens as a naval power. The throne was still unstable enough to need outside help, so Amyntas switched his allegiance to Athens in 375 B.C.E. He was again driven from the throne, but restored in 373 B.C.E., this time by Jason of Pherae, a town in Thessaly. Jason had managed to unite the whole region of Thessaly and was proclaimed Tagos (or commander) of the Thessalian League. When Jason was assassinated the next year, however, Amyntas switched back to Athens.

Amyntas' reign was thus a sorry tale, but when he died in 370 B.C.E., he at least passed the title of the kingdom on to his sons. Taking into account his beginnings and the times in which he lived, it was a considerable legacy, and all his sons held his memory dear. The reign now passed to the eldest of three remarkable brothers, Alexander II. He immediately began to put things right. He laid plans for a national army with a heavy reliance on middle-class infantry hoplites drawn from the yeoman farmers as a counterbalance for the highland noble cavalry. His goal was to bring the kingdom back to the point where it had been under Archelaus.

Alexander II founded the Pezetairoi (Foot Companions) to balance out the aristocratic Hetairoi, and raised the status of the hoplite phalanx, the formation in which heavily armed infantry fought. This new army was intended to be an instrument of nationalization and centralization for the monarchy. He began to use it almost immediately, intervening in Thessaly against the tyrannical ruling house of Pherae. But Pherae called in aid from Thebes, and Alexander's fledgling force was defeated. He was forced into an alliance with Thebes, with his brother Philip, now fourteen years old, sent as a hostage to Thebes.

In 368 B.C.E., Alexander II was assassinated by his brother-in-law, Ptolemy, at a religious festival. Ptolemy was named regent for the second son of Amyntas, Perdikkas III, but soon took the title for himself. The young Philip, now sixteen or seventeen years old, returned to Macedonia in a new exchange of hostages. In 365 B.C.E., the two brothers killed Ptolemy, and now Perdikkas III became the sole ruler. He immediately returned to the policies of Alexander II. He continued an anti-Athenian policy as well.

Alexander's military reforms were carried forward with Philip as drillmaster. Philip had spent his time in Thebes studying the new tactics employed by Thebes' great generals, Pelopidas and Epaminondas. This involved the strategy of using combined arms, cavalry and light- and heavy-armed infantry used in coordination on the battlefield rather than just the heavy hoplite maneuvers. This was an approach Philip passed on to his son, Alexander the Great. A phalanx of some 7000 to 8000 men was formed, which, added to the excellent Macedonian cavalry, made the kingdom a very powerful force in Greece. The traditional Macedonian weapon on horseback had been the sarissa, an eighteen-foot pike, which speaks volumes to the Macedonians' ability when one realizes they wielded this from horseback without the use of stirrups. Philip now introduced this weapon into the infantry formations, whereas the traditional Greek spear was only six to eight feet long. This gave Philip's new formation a considerable edge.

Feeling a growing confidence, Perdikkas stopped paying the Illyrians tribute. After turning back minor raids in 361 and 360 B.C.E., he decided to go on the offensive. In 359 B.C.E., Perdikkas took the new army into the Illyrian homeland. There, somewhere in the central Pindus, he met the Illyrians under their new chieftain, Bardyllis. The Illyrians overwhelmed the king's forces; Perdikkas and some 4000 of his men now lay dead in upper Macedonia. To succeed him, there were only an infant son named Amyntas, for his grandfather, and Philip, now aged twenty-two or twenty-three. It was no time for a child king.

Indeed, a deluge of enemies and troubles now flooded down onto the Argead kingdom. The highland chieftains threw in with Bardyllis, in part because they thought they saw an opportunity for independence, but also simply to maintain themselves. The Paeonians invaded from the north, as did the Pelagonians under their chief Menelaus. Berisades, the king of the western Thracians, came into Macedonia with a rival candidate for the Argead throne in tow. Meanwhile, the Chalcidic League became intrigued with Philip's three half brothers, sons of Amyntas III by another mother, who were also rival claimants for the throne. Finally, the Athenians landed an expeditionary force of mercenaries with Argaeus, an elderly cousin of Philip, who had for a brief time earlier been the Athenian Macedonian puppet as a rival to Amyntas III. That made for two rebellious houses and six invading forces rending the kingdom. No one would have granted odds for Macedonia's survival, but the throne had now passed to the last and most remarkable son of Amyntas III: Philip II, the father of Alexander. Everything was about to change.

I

Philip and the Young Alexander

Introduction

As of 359 B.C.E., the young king Perdikkas III and some 4000 Macedonians lay dead in highland Macedonia. The person in charge of the affairs of the kingdom was the dead king's brother, Philip, the son of Amyntas. He was faced with a host of problems: Bardyllis and his Illyrians had overrun Lynkestis and Orestis, the two westernmost tribal districts; Menelaus, the prince of Pelagonia, with the backing of Athens, had invaded from the north, as did the Paeonians; Berisades, the king of the western Odryssian Thracians, had moved into the eastern districts of Macedonia, while at the same time backing a highland prince named Pausanias as a rival for the throne. Philip's half brothers, Archelaus, Arrhidaeus, and Menelaus, were

Aegean Basin

equally intriguing for the throne, with the support of the Chalcidic League. Finally, Athens put forward, as its own candidate for the throne, Argaeus, who had briefly been a rival claimant as king during Amyntas III's time. This time Argaeus was backed by a mercenary force of 3000 sent by Athens to the city of Methone on the Macedonian coast. The odds were long for the kingdom's survival, and the chances are that Philip was chosen directly as king from the beginning (rather than as regent), since the other candidate, Perdikkas' son, Amyntas, was a child. Regardless, Philip was king in his own right by 357 B.C.E., which was a measure of his success and genius. What he did in those two years was to establish himself firmly as the greatest figure in Macedonian history.

The Struggle for Survival: 359–356 B.C.E.

At first, what Philip needed most was time and, second, more men; specifically, he needed to have time to train men to replace those who fell with Perdikkas. To gain that time and to keep his enemies at bay, Philip used a combination of bribery, persuasion, tribute, and force, all of which was calculated to keep his enemies disunited and off balance.

He bought off Berisades and the Thracians outright by bribery and even managed to have Pausanias, the pretender, killed in the bargain. Philip arranged the death of his eldest half brother, Archelaus, while his remaining two siblings fled for protection to Olynthus, the capital of the Chalcidic League. Philip paid tribute to the Paeonians, which forestalled their invasion. To gain a cadre of trained men as quickly as possible, Philip pulled out the garrison which had been protecting Amphipolis. The Illyrians and Pelagonians he could do nothing about, so he simply abandoned Orestis and Lynkestis for the time being.

By late summer, things were beginning to shape up. But then the Athenians landed their force of 3000 mercenaries and the old pretender, Argaeus, on the coast at Methone, while their fleet patrolled the Thermaic Gulf. Argaeus marched to the ancient Macedonian capital at Aegae. Philip let Argaeus do so, confident that his people would stand by Philip and not go over to the pretender. This they did, and realizing that there was no support for his candidacy, Argaeus and the mercenaries began to pull back to Methone. It was at this point that Philip struck, defeated the mercenary column, and forced them into a defensive position. Philip then bargained for the Athenian forces' safe withdrawal, the price being Argaeus and his few supporters. Athens was further neutralized by promises of peace and the renunciation of all claims to the much-coveted city of Amphipolis. The Athenians bought the proposition wholesale, and Philip had the winter of 359–358 B.C.E. to continue training his new army.

By the spring of 358 B.C.E., that army had already taken shape in the form a full hoplite phalanx, which Philip would continue to develop in size, weaponry, and tactics as time went on. In the summer, he defeated the Paeonians and Pelagonians, the latter being incorporated directly into the Macedonian state as a new tribal district. This began a process of integration, not just conquest, and it was a program to be repeated by Philip time and again. It was also to be a model for Alexander. With his right flank secure on the north, Philip then turned west against Bardyllis, using both his Macedonians and the newly acquired Pelagonian levies.

With an army of 10,000 foot and 600 cavalry, Philip marched into Lynkestis. Bardyllis tried to strike first, with an army roughly matching Philip's numbers, 10,000 foot and 500 cavalry. But Bardyllis had no hoplites to match Philip's men, and the Macedonian cavalry was far superior. As a result, Bardyllis formed up into a hollow square, as protection against the cavalry. Philip now showed what he had learned of the new tactics in Thebes. Personally leading the phalanx's right wing, Philip ordered the center and left to trail behind him in an oblique (diagonal) line. This would force the Illyrians to extend their lines just to keep contact or alternately to suffer overwhelming pressure at the initial point of contact. Either way, the Illyrians would be stretched to their limit and would eventually break the line, the entire purpose of the maneuver. Once that happened, the Macedonian cavalry was ordered to charge into the break and roll the lines up.

It worked even better than planned. Acting like a spearpoint, the Macedonian right wing broke through the Illyrian lines, followed by the cavalry. Bardyllis left 7000 dead on the field.

This tactic, and more importantly its chief purpose, to break the enemy line, or make the enemy himself break line, in order to open the way for the Macedonian cavalry, was to become the standard Macedonian practice under both Philip and Alexander. One variant or another of it would be used again by Philip at Chaeronea in 338 B.C.E. and by Alexander in his two pitched battles with the Persians under Darius III.

Bardyllis sued for peace, which he got in exchange for all of the territory up to Lake Lychnitis. Philip began to clearcut that forested area and initiated a policy of building watchtowers and frontier posts to guard against future Illyrian raids, a policy that would take years to complete. To seal the bargain, Philip took an Illyrian princess, Audata, as his wife.

In the late summer, Philip swung through Epirus, where he put Neoptolemus on the throne of the Molossi, and hence made him the leader of the Epirote League and a firm Macedonian ally against the Illyrians. Again, to seal this diplomatic bargain, he was betrothed to Neoptolemus' daughter, Myrtale, who would be the mother of Alexander the Great. The marriage took place the next spring, 357 B.C.E., and Myrtale took the name Olympias as Philip's bride. Though Macedonians followed the traditional Greek pattern of being monogamous, it is apparent from this that the Macedonian kings, evidently for reasons of state, were not. It was normal custom among the northern tribes to seal diplomatic alliances and treaties with marriage bonds. It would be a custom for Alexander as well, though not to the same degree.

Throughout the autumn, winter, and early spring of the next year, Philip continued to train his new phalanx. Now that he was secure to his north and west, he could turn his attention to his civilized neighbors: Athens and the Chalcidic League. Both were more concerned with each other than with Macedonia, especially considering its record of discord and weakness over the previous four decades. The key bone of contention was the status of Amphipolis and its control of the timber and the gold and silver deposits around it. When Philip withdrew the Macedonian garrison, he had left the city to its own devices as a free state. Athens wanted it, at least as an ally, and at best as a possession. The Chalcidic League sought to prevent this in any way possible in order to block any growth of Athenian power in the north.

Philip stepped in at this point and offered Athens help in getting Amphipolis, if they would give him a free hand against Pydna, one of two cities allied to Athens on the Macedonian coast in Pieria, the other being Methone. The opportunity was too good for Athens to pass up, and they accepted what the sources refer to as a secret pact to this effect, since one could hardly advertise the betrayal of an ally. Some word of what was up did leak out, as it is virtually impossible for a democracy to keep secrets of this sort effectively, but the leak may have been even more to Philip's advantage, and hence he may have been its source. Either way, word of such a pact was enough to prevent any preemptive strike by the Chalcidic League.

Athens, in any event, was entangled in a war with its own allies (the "Social War") fought over the control of her alliance system, the Second Confederation. As a result, they were content to let Philip act alone against Amphipolis, thinking that it was on her behalf that he was involved to begin with. Philip moved to besiege Amphipolis and, by the end of the summer of 357 B.C.E., it looked as if he would succeed. To prevent this, the Chalcidic League reversed itself and offered an alliance to Athens, which was declined because Athens presumed Philip was working for them. By autumn, the city fell to assault, but Philip freed the city and established a democracy, which promptly exiled the pro-Athenian party, to the delight of the Chalcidians.

Philip turned immediately to Pydna, where the pro-Macedonian party opened the gates to him, so the city fell without a blow. Philip put garrisons in both Amphipolis and Pydna to guarantee them against Athenian assault. There was nothing Athens could do, certainly not point to any agreement that demonstrated her betrayal of an ally. War was declared against Philip, but Athens was too tied up in the Social War, which they were in the process of losing, to do anything about it. But they did not forget that they had been outsmarted by Philip.

In the course of a little over two years, Philip had proved victorious on every front. The Illyrians had been defeated and driven back. Lynkestis and Orestis had been reincorporated into the kingdom. The Pelagonians had been defeated and assimilated into Macedonia, while the Paeonians were also beaten back. An alliance had been established with the Epirotes; a pro-Macedonian party was in control of Amphipolis and its independence from outside Greek influence guaranteed. Philip had even retaken the city of Pydna without bloodshed, in a move to reestablish Macedonian sovereignty along its own coasts. He had trained an army of hoplites, capable of facing both barbarian and civilized enemies, and given it four significant victories. The kingdom had been brought back to the stage it had achieved under Archelaus, five decades before. Most importantly, Philip had won the hearts of his people and begun the process of forging them from tribal factions into a single people. But would it last?

The Restoration of Macedonian Power (356–354 B.C.E.)

For the next few years, Philip was still primarily concerned with the security of the kingdom, reasserting control over all previously held Macedonian territory, such as Methone, and restoring Macedonian prominence to the stage it had been under Alexander I. But now he could move more aggressively. The basic policies had been set and these comprised military action against the tribal north coupled with population settlements and development. Against the southern Greek enemies, Philip used their own ambitions and greed against them, employing military force sparingly but at decisive points.

Toward that end, he made a defensive alliance with the Chalcidic League, which had become a power in its own right in the region. It could muster 10,000 hoplites and 1000 cavalry, and as such constituted a greater threat than Athens because it was nearer. Philip offered them the agriculturally rich Anthemous region just above the Chalcidic Peninsula and help in recovering the city of Potidaea from Athens, in exchange for an alliance he knew was useless, since the League had refused to honor similar commitments to Philip's father. What it did secure was their neutrality. Likewise, as his brother Alexander had done, Philip moved into Thessalian affairs, entering into a marriage alliance with the noble house of the Aleuadai of Larissa by marrying Philinna, a daughter of the house. This secured the southern passes into Macedonia.

Philip was now at least temporarily secure to the south, west, and north, and on his right flank, Chalcidice, for any move eastward. This was precisely what he had in mind: moving further east beyond Amphipolis into the plain of Drama. Again this becomes standard policy for Philip. Any time he had a free hand, that is, no threats from the surrounding tribes or entanglements with southern Greek affairs, Philip moved east into Thrace. The recently founded city of Crenides opened its gates to him. Philip renamed it Philippi, fortified it and settled a mixed population of Thracians, Macedonians, and Greeks into it. He incorporated it directly into the kingdom. This also secured a steady source of gold and silver from the mines of the region and Mount Pangeion. Philip's policies of development were costly, as was his diplomacy, and this became his primary source of seed money.

But this was not mere conquest. Philip was serious about incorporating the people as well as the region into the Macedonian kingdom itself. A decree from early in Alexander the Great's reign shows how far this integration into the kingdom went. In 336 B.C.E., some Thracian farmers had petitioned Alexander over a land dispute with Greek townsmen around Philippi and referred to a previous ruling in court from Philip which had found in their favor. Alexander reaffirmed this ruling in the decree. The interesting point was that the Thracians sought redress through the Macedonian legal system as a regular matter, expecting and receiving justice as Macedonian citizens. This will later be echoed in Alexander the Great's policies in the East as well.

The move was not without its consequences. It prompted a new alliance of northern tribes against Philip: Grabus, who had replaced Bardyllis in Illyria; Lyppeus of Paeonia; and Cetriporus of Thrace. Philip campaigned here himself, and equally used his trusted generals, Parmenio and Antipater, as independent commanders, blanketing the tribal alliance. Philip defeated his enemies piecemeal, never letting them unite. In the summer of 356 B.C.E., while besieging Potidaea, his price for continued Chalcidic neutrality, Philip received word on the same day of three great events. Parmenio had defeated Grabus; his horses had won the premier chariot race at the Olympics; and Olympias had borne him a son, whom he named for his favorite brother, Alexander. His next act, so as not to make the gods jealous, was to throw his favorite ring into the sea!

By 354 B.C.E., Philip completed the recovery of the kingdom by taking the city of Methone, though he lost an eye in the assault. Philip had not only restored the kingdom, but he had already begun its eastward expansion; secured revenues to cover his widespread economic development; built up his army; and provided the stability of an heir to his throne.

Nation Building: the Nature of Philip's Kingdom

There is a tendency in studying Philip to concentrate primarily on his relations with the Greeks (because our Greek sources themselves do), which ironically ignores his main interests: internal development of the kingdom and eastward expansion. Indeed, his whole program was meant to address the kingdom's three traditional problems: the barbaric tribes to the north, the Greeks to the south, and the internal instability caused by the highland principalities. His goal was to create one kingdom and one people from all of these elements, and the chief instrument for doing so was to be a national army. The idea behind this was not simply to overawe these three factors, though the army would obviously be useful in that regard. But Philip was more subtle than that. As Macedonians from all districts and ethnic groups served together, they also came to know one another, to trust one another, and to think of themselves as one people. Even more important, as Philip led them to victory after victory, they looked to him and the Argead house (rather than their tribal chiefs) as the source of security, unity, prosperity, and development.

It was not unlike the effect that the veterans of the Continental Army had on the concept of a federal union and the debate that created the Constitution of the United States. They too had marched together, fought together for the idea of freedom, and so saw beyond their own states' borders. Given, however, that we are talking about a kingdom, in what will ultimately become an almost global perspective, an even more apt comparison would be the manner in which Genghis Khan built an empire from the tribes of Mongolia.

The military program took years to complete, and its importance for us is that it was Philip's legacy to Alexander the Great. So it will be easier and more useful to look at Macedonia at the end of that process, that is, by the end of Philip's reign in 336 B.C.E. This will provide our first look at what will later be Alexander's army, and the best time to discuss the nature of that army.

For recruitment and administrative purposes, Philip divided the kingdom into ten tribal cantons, largely but not exclusively based on the traditional districts. In terms of the national army, each of these cantons supplied a 1500-man hoplite brigade (*taxsis*) to Philip annually. This meant Philip could rely on ten territorial brigades amounting to 15,000 heavy infantrymen.

Judging from the troop numbers during Alexander the Great's reign, Alexander took with him in the Persian campaign, or later received piecemeal in reinforcements, a total of some 60,000 Macedonians. Another 15,000 men of military age were left at home under the trusted general and regent Antipater to defend the kingdom. The sources make clear these were largely old men and boys left at home, so the overall number of 75,000 represented all the kingdom could muster. From this one can deduce that Philip never called on more than 20 percent of his full resources at any one time for his military campaigns. The remainder stayed in Macedonia to tend their farms and defend the kingdom.

Philip probably rotated the men in these brigades so that everyone had the chance of serving. This fulfilled several functions: It spread both the burden of service and opportunity for booty equally; it meant that all Macedonians learned to fight alongside their fellow citizens from different areas of the kingdom, and so developed a national consciousness of being Macedonians; and it meant that they all had a chance personally to see Philip as their king. At first, these units were commanded by their traditional tribal chieftains, but over time Philip moved the commanders around to mix them up deliberately. Again the point was to create a national identity rather than a tribal one, and this served to break down the highland chiefs' control of their home areas as well.

Philip was innovative in more than recruitment. These hoplites were not armed in the traditional heavy infantry manner. They carried smaller, lighter shields, and only light body armor, but were equipped with a heavier striking weapon: the traditional Macedonian pike, the sarissa. Previously, this had been used only by the Macedonian cavalry, but now the infantry was trained in its use as well. The sarissa was an 18-foot weapon consisting of two cornel wood shafts held together by an iron sleeve. It was topped with a pikehead larger than the normal Greek spear and balanced with a weighted buttspike at the other end. The purpose was to balance the entire weapon so it would be easier to wield, but also to make it easy to break down for transport. In the event the shaft was shattered, the buttspike could be used for self defense as a mace or club. In a Macedonian phalanx formation, five pikeheads would project between each man in the front line, creating a hedge of spearpoints. The normal Greek hoplite formation carried spears of no more than eight feet, and only two spearpoints would project between each man in the front rank. The Greeks wore heavier body armor, which made their formations slower and more unwieldy than the Macedonians.

Philip, however, did not abandon the traditional Greek spear or formation. Men were trained in the use of both, as well as with the small target shield (*pelta*) and javelins. All arms would be carried with the army, and units were equipped as Philip saw fit depending on the terrain, the kind of enemy to be faced, and the sorts of allies and mercenaries available. The whole point of the formation was speed and flexibility.

Generally in the Greek world, phalanx formations customarily ranged from eight to sixteen ranks deep, though the Thebans and others experimented with even deeper variations. The length of the line depended on the number of available men overall in the phalanx, and the terrain on which they fought. This essentially was flat plainsland, tight formations being impossible on broken ground. Philip's formations, on the other hand, were more open and flexible because of the lighter shield and armor as well as varied uses and weapons. As a result, the Macedonian phalanx, while at its best on flat ground, could operate on mildly rough territory. Taken together with cavalry and light armed troops in combined and coordinated tactics, it could fight on practically any ground whatsoever, as both Philip and Alexander were to prove.

In addition to the territorial brigades, Philip had his own standing force: a Guards Brigade called the Hypaspists (the Longshields). This consisted of a permanent standing force of three regiments of 1000 men each (called a chiliarchy in Greek). The lead regiment was named the Agema, the King's Own, because it was personally led by him. These were, heart and soul, king's men. Philip chose them, trained them, and preferred to fight with them in pitched battles. They probably corresponded to the old Pezetairoi or Foot Companions. It should not escape notice that they were equal in numbers to any two territorial brigades; but where the latter were militia, the Longshields were professionals. Even more important, when taking the highland units into account, the three heartland cantons, Pieria, Bottiaia, and Eordaia, always made up another 4500 men in the army. This meant there was a solid corps, even from the beginning, on whom Philip could rely utterly.

In terms of the cavalry for which Macedonia had always been famed, each canton provided a

300-man territorial cavalry squadron (called a hipparchy) to the national army. This gave Philip 3000 of the best horsemen in Greece. To this he added the old Horse Companions (*Hetairoi*) who had always supported the Argead king. These amounted to between 1200 and 2000 men. The lead squadron of the Companions was also called the Agema, and it was this unit that Alexander preferred to command in battle. As with the infantry brigades, Philip rotated both the service in and command of the territorial squadrons in order to break down regional prejudices. All command appointments within the army came from the ranks of Hetairoi, which insured the loyalty of Philip's officers.

So overall, Philip could count on a preponderance of excellent cavalry, which even internally (counting the heartland territorial squadrons) came to between 2100 to 2900 men and outnumbered any combination from the highland areas as well. For these obvious reasons, there were no highland rebellions in Philip's reign after 357 B.C.E., but as we shall see, there were even more cogent reasons for this. For now, note that this gave Philip a Macedonian army of 18,000 heavy infantry and 5000 cavalry which he could use against any external foe at any time, while still defending the kingdom from barbarian raids and keeping the economy productive. In previous

Iron corselet (thorax) from Tomb II at Vergina. The corselet imitates the normal stiffened linen cuirass worn by Greco-Macedonian soldiers in the fourth century. Most of the artifacts from Vergina are now housed in a new museum at the site itself. (Photograph by Winthrop Lindsay Adams, taken at the Archaeological Museum at Thessaloniki.)

centuries, at the height of Sparta's power, she herself could field an army of no more than 10,000; and in the fifth century, at the apex of her power, Athens had an army of only 12,000 hoplites. The implications of this for Macedonia were clear; Philip had made her the single most powerful state in the Greek peninsula.

Philip's armies, however, were in fact even larger than this. First, as with most Greek states, he employed mercenaries as specialized troops. These were mostly used as light armed infantry in the case of Macedonia, though other states employed hoplite mercenaries as well. For example, Persia had some 60,000 Greek hoplite mercenaries in her pay at the time of Alexander's invasion. Philip hired Cretan archers, renowned for their specialty, as well as slingers, javelinmen, and peltasts from the northern barbarian tribes. In the case of the tribal mercenaries, this served two purposes: These troops were very good, and by paying them and draining off their energy and excess population, Philip eased tensions on his own frontiers.

Second, Philip also developed a kind of military technological think tank. A group of mechanical engineers, under a Thessalian named Polyidus, worked for Philip. These included Diades and Charias, who were later to serve with distinction under Alexander. This group developed new and highly portable siege equipment including catapults, stonethrowers, and siege towers. Up to this point, when trying to take a city, an army would build towers, ladders and catapults out of local material, and then abandon them when the siege ended. That meant the effectiveness of the weapons varied greatly. It is hardly a surprise that most cities were either betrayed from within or starved into submission rather than taken by assault.

Catapults, down to the generation before Philip, had consisted of weight-throwing weapons which relied on the tensile strength of a tree trunk or a laminated throwing arm which was bent back. When released, the arm would fly up and hit an arresting bar, while the material being hurled would continue on against the target. It was neither accurate nor very powerful, certainly not powerful enough to batter down a stone wall.

In 398 B.C.E., on the island of Sicily, Dionysius of Syracuse introduced the use of the torsion catapult. In this case, the throwing arm was placed in a cable tier of rope (usually made from horsehair) twisted tautly from top to bottom. Then the single arm (or two arms in a device resembling a large crossbow) was winched back, and the throwing strength came from the torque in the cable tier rather than the arm itself. This greatly increased the power and accuracy of the weapon. A catapult normally fires an arrow, which could range from one to six feet in length. In the hands of an experienced gunner, a catapult could hit an individual target at 100 yards (far more accurate than a smoothbore musket even up to the American Civil War). It could hit a group of men at up to 400 or 500 yards, and had an extreme range of 700 yards, although power and accuracy declined. The problem was that it was cumbersome, the crew had to be protected

PHILIP AND THE YOUNG ALEXANDER + 57

from attack, and the rate of fire was slow. The result was that it was generally not an effective weapon on the battlefield. Alexander would devise a method of using it like artillery on a couple of occasions to cover hostile river crossings, but it would not be until the time of the Romans that it became a regular feature on the battlefield itself.

The other type of siege weapon was a *petrobolos,* or stonethrower. Using the same form of torsion propulsion and same general construction, a stonethrower could hurl a half-talent weight (around 25 pounds or 13 kilograms) about 400 yards, and a full talent (around 50 pounds or 26 kilograms) about 150 yards with great accuracy. In the early modern European era, the French military architect Vauban considered catapults more accurate than cannons for specialty work, though obviously not as powerful. Such a weapon could hammer at a stonewall until it caused a breach and permit an assault on the city or fortification without having to waste large numbers of men in a ladder- or tower-born attack intended to carry the wall at the top. It could also be fitted to hurl jars filled with burning oil and other nasty items. Alexander would eventually develop a knack for siege warfare, using both these weapons and ingenious infantry tactics.

Down to Philip's time, torsion catapults had been seen only in Greece proper as a kind of curiosity. Now he made them a mainstay of both land and naval warfare. In fact, Philip developed a complete engineering department. Engineering specialists accompanied the army, with the components for these machines broken down for transport.

Equally innovative, Philip had a regular medical service to treat the wounded on the field itself and after the battle. Prior to this the wounded were tended by friends, while the severely injured were simply killed as an act of mercy. Though begun by Philip, it is likely that this was another major development by Alexander. Later on, Alexander was regularly seen in the sources going among the wounded in hospital following major engagements and took a keen interest in medicine. This is hardly surprising since Alexander was a student of Aristotle, whose original training had been as a physician.

The overall result was that Philip had not only a large military force, but the first real army in the Western tradition, that is a complete fighting force with integrated units, necessary support services, and staff. Other examples of this kind of force had long been in evidence in the ancient Near East among the Egyptians, the Assyrians, and the Persians. But also note that the innovations in artillery, engineering, and medical service by Philip and Alexander were designed to take care of their men. The manner in which the army was constituted, and its use of technology, had more than just military ramifications. These reforms also had social, political, and economic consequences.

The socialization aspect of this process along with the organization of the army fostered a Macedonian consciousness. Politically, in the Macedonian tradition, the army had always constituted a national assembly, as it did in the rest of Greece. They had a role in choosing the kings and in trying, judging, and punishing traitor, and a right to address the king, singly or in groups, by petition in circumstances that others (especially the Romans) would consider mutinous. The Greeks considered this free speech *(isegoria)*. It is also likely that Philip now used the assembly more often to pass laws and endorse his policies. In short, he used it as a democratic instrument of self-government. This was equally aimed at breaking any aristocratic power previously exercised by the highland princes and chieftains by submerging them in a national assembly. It also involved average Macedonians in Philip's programs and allowed them to make decisions as citizens and partners, not as subjects. It served to encourage the Macedonians to think of themselves as one people and no longer a cluster of tribal factions. This was recognized even by the southern Greek city-states. Where it was normal for Greeks to refer to the subjects of kings as *douloi* or slaves, that term is never applied to the Macedonians.

Finally, rounding out the social and economic developments, Philip used several polices that all worked together toward the same ends of integration and national unity. As he moved eastward, and established the western and northern frontiers as well, Philip founded cities on the periphery. This was partially to provide needed defense points against the wilder tribes beyond, and partially to facilitate socialization. Judging from our sources and the names chosen for these new cities, this involved large movement of populations from the interior. Lowlanders were settled in the highlands, in towns alongside both highland Macedonians and people from other local ethnic groups. At the same time, especially as he incorporated areas in Thrace, Philip moved highland and lowland Macedonians into new towns alongside Thracians. Always using mixed populations in these settlements, Philip was not only mixing the two native Macedonian elements together, but giving land to the Thracians in the context of city foundations on the frontiers. This fulfilled the Macedonian definition of citizenship, holding land from the king in exchange for military service, and thus enfranchised these peoples as Macedonian citizens regardless of their ethnic origins.

This process might have meant a gradual depopulation of the heartland region of Macedonia, except that Philip made provision for that as well. Non-Macedonian ethnic groups from the frontiers were settled in the heartland in large numbers. For instance, following a campaign late in his reign against the Scythian king Atheas, Philip resettled some 20,000 Scythians to the interior of Macedonia. By giving them land and making them liable for recruitment, Philip was in fact making Macedonians of them. Indeed, our source for this, Justin, says that it was precisely in this manner that Philip "from many peoples and tribes made one kingdom and one people."

Hand in hand with this went the economic development of these regions, as a necessary support for the new foundations. Marshes were drained for farms and stockraising. Vineyards, orchards, and olive groves were planted, and their produce marketed. The natural resources were exploited: Mines were opened and forests harvested. The cities established became trading points for finished goods into the upper Balkans, as well as transport centers for raw materials out from the region. This was facilitated by the introduction of a new coinage designed to be the standard economic unit of trade for the entire region. It was modeled after the Persian coin, the gold daric, but called the philippic for obvious reasons.

The task in which Philip was engaged is what we would call state building. He was creating a nation with an integrated population, a national economy, national political institutions, and, coincidentally, an army. It is too easy to concentrate on this last point alone, as most sources do. All during his reign, this is what was going on in Macedonia internally and along all the barbarian frontiers (as opposed to Philip's relations with the Greeks). In the best ancient source on Alexander, the history of Arrian, the author has Alexander make a major speech to his Macedonians which sums all of this up nicely:

> "Let me begin with Philip, as I properly should. For Philip found you wandering and helpless, garbed in sheepskins, pasturing your few flocks on the hillside, and doing badly against the Illyrians, Triballi, and Thracians on your frontiers. Philip gave you cloaks to wear instead of sheepskins; brought you down from the mountains to the plains; made you victorious over your neighbors so that you trusted your own courage rather than the strength of your village [walls]. No, he made you the inhabitants of cities; gave you good laws and customs. He made you masters rather than slaves."

Philip and the Greeks

Philip's attention was drawn to Greek affairs in the south almost as soon as he had completed the restoration of the kingdom with the reconquest of Methone. His relationship with the Greek states and settlement in the south will be of prime importance to Alexander. First, Philip paved the way for Alexander, whose own relationship with the Greeks will be defined by it. Second, the form and function of Alexander's alliance against Persia was the result of Philip's labors and ideas.

In the same year that Alexander was born, 356 B.C.E., a war broke out in Greece which came to involve almost all the Greek states to one degree or another. It revolved around the site of the Oracle of Apollo at Delphi in Phocis (central Greece). This site was sacred to all Greeks, Macedonians included. It was protected and administered by the only truly panhellenic institution, a religious league called the Delphic Amphictyony, and its Council. The Amphictony's purpose was to guarantee access to Delphi for all Greeks. Most states maintained treasuries at Delphi to house their dedications to Apollo, and as a result it had developed as a banking center as well. When the Thebans threatened the conquest of the area in 356 B.C.E. the Phocians seized these assets as their only hope to survive. Using these funds, they equipped themselves and hired a large mercenary force to defend Phocis. Almost overnight they became a major force in Greece.

It worked, and Thebes was stopped in its tracks, but as an act against the temple of Apollo, it was a sacrilege. The Thebans brought this to the Council, which condemned the act and declared a Sacred War to avenge themselves on Phocis. All Greece was split into the supporters of Thebes, mostly the cities of Thessaly (which had ten out of the eighteen votes on the Council) in one camp; and the Phocians backed by Thebes' enemies, particularly Athens and Sparta, in the other. The nature of the war precluded a negotiated settlement (there could be no quarter given in a Sacred War and so no way to resolve it except victory for one side or the other). Further, the ritual punishment proposed for Phocis was virtual genocide: Every man and boy was to be killed; every woman and child sold into slavery; and their towns razed to the ground. It would amount to what is referred to today as ethnic cleansing. Finally, both sides were so evenly balanced that no decisive resolution was available on the field of battle. The war simply continued.

Philip was drawn into this war because of his support for the cities in northern Thessaly, which protected the southern passes into Macedonia.

He also genuinely supported the Council, and was a devotee of the Oracle of Apollo. The Thessalian army was defeated by the Phocians in early 354 B.C.E. and Philip intervened to protect them, winning a victory at Neon on the southern border of Thessaly. A fresh army from Phocis, with the support of the Thessalian towns of Pherae and Crannon, moved back into the region the next year. Move prompted counter move. Leading a combined army of Macedonians and Thessalians amounting to 20,000 hoplites and 3000 cavalry, Philip won a decisive engagement at the Battle of the Crocus Fields in 352 B.C.E. As a result, a now-united Thessaly chose Philip as the Tagos, or commander, of the Thessalian League, which gave him control of all Thessalian forces. Philip, however, did not annex a single square foot of Thessalian territory. All Thessalian cities remained autonomous. It was a simple acknowledgement that Philip was their only guarantee against invasion. For his part, following the victory, Philip turned his attentions back to the internal development of Macedon and its expansion eastward into Thrace, his real interest. He moved the borders of the kingdom to the Hebrus River, the current border between Greece and Turkey.

In moving east, Philip saw Athens, with its commercial interests in the north and its Black Sea trade, as a threat to that continued expansion.

Though the fighting in the Third Sacred War had now degenerated into guerilla warfare, Athens was allied to Phocis. Philip countered this by working with those northern cities of the Aegean, like Byzantium, which were opposed to Athens. The growth of Philip's power was so recent, and the history of Macedonian weakness so prevalent that Athens, and especially its most influential leader, Demosthenes, did not recognize Philip as a serious threat. Demosthenes thought that Philip could be dealt with by counter alliances and backing northern barbarian tribes like the Thracians, which had been Athenian policy for over a century.

But when Philip began to build a fleet in 350 B.C.E., it caught Athens off guard. The next year the Macedonian fleet raided Athenian shipping and even landed at Marathon in Attica itself. Now Demosthenes and Athens took notice. In the "First Philippic" (a speech delivered against Philip), Demosthenes urged an immediate attack on Philip, whom he compared to a boxer: one who was quick and resilient; one whose blows were always parried too late. It was a good characterization, and Demosthenes was to say worse.

Athens needed bases in the north, and the obvious ally to further her war against Philip was the Chalcidic League, sitting on Philip's right flank. Unfortunately for them, it was obvious to Philip as well. Olynthus, the capital of the League, had granted asylum to Philip's remaining half brothers, Arrhidaeus and Menelaus, who still maintained their claim to the Macedonian throne. In 349 B.C.E., Philip issued a demand for the brothers' return, and its refusal would amount to a declaration of war. Demosthenes, in three successive speeches, the "Olynthiacs," urged action on Athens, but Philip had timed things well. His first moves came in late November or early December, when the stiff seasonal north wind, the Bora, hindered rapid movement by the Athenians. In one jump, he seized all of the Chalcidic peninsula and besieged Olynthus. The next year, in a pitched battle before the city, the Olynthians deserted to Philip. The whole area was incorporated into Macedonia in the same fashion that Thrace and the frontiers had been. Macedonians were settled into "refounded towns" which were also used as instruments of enfranchisement for the non-ethnic Macedonian population. The entire north was now securely Macedonian, and Philip again turned his attention further eastward.

In the autumn of 348 B.C.E., Philip opened negotiations with Athens for peace and alliance, an offer not accepted. Philip renewed his interest in the Third Sacred War in the next year, and by 346 B.C.E. Philip had moved an army to Thermopylae, the gateway to central Greece, held by the Phocians. Philip again tried to renew negotiations with Athens through their envoy Philocrates, who convinced the Athenians to accept both peace and alliance. Philip then moved to end the Third Sacred War by offering to accept the Phocians surrender and promising not to carry out the ritual punishment.

Taking what has been called the Peace of Philocrates as the basis, Philip now established a diplomatic settlement for all of Greece based on peace and homonoia (equality). Each state pledged peace and fair treatment. As Tagos of the Thessalian League, Philip controlled ten out of the eighteen votes on the Council of the Delphic Amphictyony. This assured Philip that his leniency to the Phocians would be upheld under the *homonoia* clause of the final treaty. Their punishment was to cede their two votes on the Council to Philip personally and to repay the monies seized in the war. Nothing else was done to them. Philip hoped that the Council would become the forum to resolve disputes in Greece, rather than relying on force of arms. For the next six years he worked toward that end. Not one square foot of Greek territory was annexed; all Greek cities remained autonomous in what was clearly a diplomatic, not a military settlement. His hands freed from Greek troubles, Philip once again turned his attention to the internal development of Macedonia and eastward expansion.

Things are never that simple. The main thrust of Greek politics for more than a century had been the tension between the larger states, who wanted to unite the smaller states under them, and the desire of every Greek city, on the other hand, to keep its own freedom and autonomy. Any possibility of unification under a larger city threatened the others' sense of independence. It was this threat which saw Greece follow Sparta in destroying the Athenian empire at the end of the fifth century in the Peloponnesian War. The effect of that was only to have the former enemies and allies of Sparta join together to put an end to her threatened hegemony. In turn, Thebes suffered the same fate in the middle of the fourth century when she tried to unify Greece. It was now Philip's turn.

Further, as long as Philip's system remained in effect, Athens' own ambitions to rebuild her empire were blocked. Demosthenes was the chief Athenian spokesman for their policy to weaken the peace settlement and Philip's position. By 344 B.C.E., he was the head of a commission to counteract Philip's influence in the other states of Greece, even though such an action went against the equality clause of the peace and directly against Athens' pledges as an ally of Philip. When states such as Argos made public what Demosthenes was doing, he hurried back to Athens. Philip merely protested diplomatically the Athenian actions against him. Demosthenes' answer was to continue attacking Philip in his speeches, frequently on the basis of a personal smear campaign. He also made the Athenian claim to all the territory they had once held in the north and which was now part of Macedonia.

Over the next four years relations continued to deteriorate. Philip carried out his internal policies in Macedonia, and his expansion into Thrace. By the spring of 342 B.C.E., Athens was directly involved against Philip, despite the peace and her formal alliance to him. Athenian vessels began taking Macedonian merchantmen at sea; Athenian mercenaries attacked Macedonian allies in the north and conducted slave raids in Thrace. When Philip sent an envoy to protest, the ambassador was seized and held for ransom. Philip protested and even offered arbitration, and Demosthenes' answer in "On the Chersonese" and the "Third Philippic" was to tell the crowd to beat to death any advocate of peace.

By 340 B.C.E., Philip was fed up. He had been campaigning against Byzantium and Perinthus for most of that season and had left the sixteen-year-old Alexander as regent in Macedonia, where he and Philip's two most trusted generals, Antipater and Parmenio, campaigned on the northern frontier to protect Philip's left flank. Philip returned to Macedonia, and to prevent any interference along his barbarian frontiers, he and Alexander campaigned up into the central Balkans all the next year. Athens convinced other Greek states such as Thebes, angry over the peaceful settlement of the Third Sacred War, to join them in an alliance.

In the spring of 338 B.C.E., Philip moved south and the decisive battle of Greek history was fought about 30 kilometers from Thebes at a place called Chaeronea. Commanding an army of 30,000 hoplites and 2000 cavalry, Philip was faced by a Greek allied force of 35,000 infantry, including 10,000 Athenians, and likewise 2000 cavalry. The allies took up positions in front of the Kerata Pass, with the Thebans on the right, the other central Greek cities in the middle, and Athens on the left. Philip, commanding the Longshields, took the Macedonian right opposite Athens. Alexander, aged eighteen, commanded the Companion Cavalry.

As he had done against Bardyllis, Philip had the line strung diagonally to his left with the center and left trailing him. That meant he came in contact with the Athenians first. The point was to break the Greek line, and Alexander had orders to charge the gap when that happened. But instead of pressing forward, Philip deliberately pulled his right wing back up the slight rise behind him while the rest of the line kept in contact. The Athenians thought he was retreating and broke lines to pursue. That opened the gap for Alexander. He charged into it while Philip turned on the Athenians. Alexander rolled up the allied Greek line. The Athenians, caught and exposed in the open, fled up the Kerata Pass.

Demosthenes told Athens to brace for an invasion. Instead, Philip sent the young Alexander as his ambassador, returning the prisoners taken at Chaeronea (without ransom) and the ashes of the Athenian dead from the battle, escorted by a guard of honor. Philip promised not to invade Athenian territory and merely asked for another formal alliance. It was a characteristic gesture by Philip, and it brought a letter from the Athenian orator Isocrates. For fifty years, Isocrates had been urging the Greek states to settle their differences and to make common cause against the Persians, whose gold had been fueling the perpetual state of war in Greece since the Peloponnesian War at the end of the fifth century. Isocrates now asked Philip "to put an end to the madness and greed with which the Greeks have treated one another, and bring them into *homonoia*; and declare war on Persia." It was to this task that Philip now turned.

The League of Corinth and the Death of Philip

Philip spent the remainder of the summer and autumn after Chaeronea settling disputes and making a triumphal progress through Greece. He summoned those interested states to send delegates to a meeting in Corinth in the spring of 337 B.C.E. to discuss a plan to establish *homonoia* and take up Isocrates' challenge. Philip had already tried to do this once, of course, through the Delphic Amphictyony, the failure of which had led to the battlefield of Chaeronea. Philip had in mind something which, if not entirely new, was at least a combination of those things that had been successful in the past. What emerged was a political and military alliance, designed as a guarantee to the political autonomy of its members, with a collective security arrangement and provisions for resolving disputes. But most important, its primary function was to forge a military coalition against Persia.

Our Greek sources (which include a partial copy of the decree itself) call this simply the alliance of Philip and the Greeks, though modern historians refer to it as the League of Corinth or the Hellenic League. It was not an attempt to unify Greece, though some scholars have tried to stretch it into that. There were no provisions for an economic union or standards set for coinage, weights, and measures which would be necessary for that. There was no common legal system or set of laws established. There was no creation of a common league citizenship, nor the acknowledgment of any common religious site as a symbol. All of these had been used in one fashion or another by other Greek alliances in the past. Nothing of the sort was attempted here.

It was strictly a political and military entity which established a partnership between Philip, on the one hand, and all of the Greeks on the other, with the exception of Sparta which refused to join on the grounds she "was accustomed to lead the Greeks." It did establish a Koine Eirene (Common Peace) among its members. It provided for a League Council, or Synedrion, in which each state was represented on a proportional basis in relation to the size of the military contingent it supplied to the League forces. In this regard, every state was to have at least one, but not more than ten representatives in the Synedrion. It is one of the first known examples of proportional representation in Western history. An executive board of five members was to be elected by the Council to preside over the League, no more than one from any given state. That Council chose Philip to be *hegemon*, or captain general of Greece, to lead the League forces. On his own behalf, Philip, meaning Macedonia, would match the League forces in any campaign.

Each member state swore an oath to remain loyal to the Koine Eirene and to the alliance with Philip. They promised to abstain from attacking any member state who observed these oaths; to refrain from the hostile occupation of any city, fort, or harbor belonging to a member state. They pledged not to attempt in any way to subvert the kingdom of Philip and his descendants, which had been among Athens' favorite pastimes for more than a century, and clearly that was part of the advantage of the alliance for Philip. They would not undermine the constitution that existed in any member state at the time the oaths were taken, which thereby guaranteed the autonomy of each state. They explicitly promised to do nothing to undermine the treaty that established the League and to prevent others from doing so. In the event of any infraction, the member states would assist the injured party and punish the offender "in accordance with the decision of the Synedrion." These provisions are not unlike the United Nations Charter, but in this case made up of Greek states.

The initial Council was made up of 100 members, and it was scheduled to meet annually in conjunction with whichever of the four Panhellenic Games was being held that year. These were the Olympic Games in Elis, which were revived in the nineteenth century, C.E., and form the basis for our modern Olympic Games; the Pythian Games at Delphi; the Isthmian Games at Corinth; and the Nemean Games at Argos. Extraordinary meetings could be summoned as needed. The decisions of the Council were to be final, and the councilors could not be called into account by their own states after the votes, which made them fully plenipotentiary (capable of voting independently as their consciences dictated). There was a special set of four Guardians from the Council who were: 1) to guarantee that all League documents had official permanent copies recorded and preserved in both Macedonia and Greece; and 2) "to ensure that, in the participating states of the Peace, there be no acts bringing death or exile contrary to the laws of those states, no confiscation of property, no redistribution of land, no cancellation of debts, and no freeing of slaves to revolutionary ends." In short, the point was that the internal constitutions of these states were to be preserved, no civil wars would occur, and no anti-treaty witchhunts would take place.

All in all, it was a remarkable agreement, much of which, except for the position on slavery, resonates quite well in our era. One should note that it was reached through debate and negotiation, not dictated. But equally, Philip's hand can be seen throughout. He had two points in its creation. The first was the alliance itself and war with Persia, and just such a declaration of war occurred at the end of the Council meeting of

337 B.C.E., a war Alexander inherited. The second was to provide for a peaceful Greece to be left behind in the wake of that invasion of Persian territory, for it had been Persian policy to protect themselves by stirring up trouble in Greece and keeping the Greeks at each others' throats.

Philip ordered the allied forces to rally to his banner in the spring of 336 B.C.E. In the meantime, he sent an expeditionary force of 10,000 of his own forces under Parmenio and another Macedonian general named Attalus to seize a beachhead across the Hellespont in Asia Minor. They were to prepare for the allied invasion.

When spring of 336 B.C.E. came, Philip celebrated the marriage of his daughter, Cleopatra, to the king of the Molossi, Alexander of Epirus. Judging from later events and Alexander the Great's invasion plans, Philip's plans were for this Alexander (of Epirus) to lead a force to unite the Greeks in Italy just as he intended to do for the Greek cities along the Asia Minor coast, as a first step against Persia. However, during a religious procession at Aegae following the marriage, as Philip entered the theater, he was cut down by one of his own bodyguards who bore him a personal grudge. Ironically, he fell victim to the very act which he had worked all his life to avoid; the thing which 63 years before had plunged the kingdom into weakness and obscurity.

The measure of the work Philip had done was that the kingdom remained united. That afternoon, his army assembly proclaimed the twenty-year-old prince Alexander to be king to succeed his father. Alexander's first words were to assure everyone that the only thing that had changed was the name of the king. At last, we reach Alexander himself.

11

King Alexander

Introduction

When Philip was cut down by an assassin in the summer of 336 B.C.E., meeting the same fate as so many Argead kings, the fear of conspiracy was widespread. Though the killer had struck alone, the general belief was that he was acting in someone else's interest. A brief bloodbath ensued which left but one choice to the army assembly: that choice was the son of Philip and Olympias, Alexander, who had already proven himself in three campaigns even though he was only twenty years old. Even without the reprisals removing Alexander's possible rivals, the results would have been the same for the prince, who had led the Hetairoi to victory at Chaeronea and been voted by the army as the hero of the battle. Parmenio and Antipater,

Philip's most trusted commanders, sponsored him to the assembly and he was enthusiastically confirmed. What sort of man was he?

Alexander's Childhood and Training

Alexander's character has largely been an enigma over the centuries. His life and actions became the stuff of myth and legend even before his death, and were heavily romanticized after it. Further, where modern psychology in analyzing an individual has tended to concentrate on childish behavior and problems still present in the adult, the ancient biographical technique was the reverse. They looked for traits of the future adult in the child's behavior.

As a result, the stories of Alexander's childhood from Plutarch, for instance, are of two types. First are the acts presaging his adult interests, which have Alexander at the age of six questioning Persians about routes and resources in their country. Those should be taken with a grain of salt. The second are those stories that have some support in the general Macedonian background, or coincide with Philip's or Alexander's known activities, and which therefore ring true. It is in the *Life of Alexander* that Plutarch makes clear his method. He is not writing history ". . . but LIVES, and in the most famous actions there is not always a clear showing of virtue or vice. No, a small thing such as a phrase or a joke frequently makes a greater revelation of character than a battle where thousands fell, or the greatest tactics employed by an army or in the besieging of a city" (*Alex*. 1.2).

The old view was that Alexander inherited his passionate nature and emotions from Olympias and his brains from Philip. Aside from the fact that genetics don't work that way, any cursory study of Philip's life would reveal that he was passionate in the extreme, and that Olympias' intelligence and capability were manifest throughout her life. It does serve a purpose, however, in that it points out the dichotomy and dynamic tension of Alexander's childhood; He was continually pulled between these two strong personalities. They were the polarities of his life.

Myth comes into the story from the beginning. The marriage of Philip and Olympias had been both politically convenient and a genuine love match. When Olympias bore Philip a son, her position at court became secure. Olympias herself was not beyond using myth as propaganda to further her own position and Alexander's. Later, when Philip continued to acquire wives and favorites, Olympias spread the story that Alexander had really been conceived by Zeus in the form of a snake, a sacred animal of the Sabazius cult, of which she was high priestess, and thus Alexander had a divine nature. The Temple of Demeter at Ephesus in Asia Minor was supposedly struck by lightning, also sacred to Zeus, at the moment of Alexander's birth, and burnt to the ground, heralding Alexander's future conquest of Asia.

Olympias' stories were interesting bits of nonsense, and certainly Philip never gave them any credence. As for Alexander, even at the end of his life, he always referred to his "father, Philip." These tales clearly were circulated after Olympias began to lose favor at court and were designed to cover that loss and reinforce her own position as mother of the heir. In fact, they were monuments to Philip's patience. The Ephesus story was obviously self-serving and told purely in hindsight. There is no evidence it was spread about at the time of Alexander's birth.

In terms of Alexander's upbringing, Philip saw to it that he had a proper tutor as a child, one Leonidas. Alexander said of him much later that Leonidas' idea of a good breakfast was a long night's march. His role was to teach Alexander the self-discipline necessary for a king and commander. It was also a counterpoint to Olympias' doting influence. Alexander told the story of Leonidas going through Alexander's chests and trunks looking for sweets that Olympias gave to him, in order to take them away.

Olympias equally provided Alexander with a teacher, Lysimachus of Acarnania, who spent most of his time outrageously praising the prince and comparing him favorably to the hero of the *Iliad*, Achilles, from whom the royal house of the Molossi traced its descent. So from Leonidas, Alexander learned the virtues expected of a prince of the Argead house, and from Lysimachus, he learned to read, write, and play the lyre.

The trick in raising his son, as Philip seems to have seen it, was not to break his spirit but encourage it on the grounds that one can't teach the timid to be bold, but one can teach discipline to the adventurous. It is clear that Philip had a fierce pride in his son. The best example of this from Alexander's youth, and the most famous, is the story of Bucephalus, Alexander's favorite charger. In 346 B.C.E., when Alexander was about ten years old, a Thessalian horse dealer brought to the autumn festival of Zeus at Dion a large black stallion with a large head, intended for sale at the princely sum of thirteen talents (about 340 kilograms of silver, roughly equivalent in buying power to $13 million). Philip was always looking to improve the breeding stock for the royal herds and was attracted to the animal. But the horse balked at his handlers and fought them, so Philip decided to pass on the deal.

Alexander, though, had taken to the horse and further, had seen the problem. The grooms had positioned the horse's back to the sun, and he was literally frightened by his own shadow. Alexander announced that he could handle the animal. Seeing what appeared to be brash behavior, Philip sought to teach Alexander a lesson—stay out of your elders' affairs—and bet him the price of the horse. If Alexander tamed the horse and therefore won the wager, the horse was his; if he failed, he owed Philip thirteen talents of silver. Alexander put a blanket over the stallion's head and turned him into the sun so he wouldn't see his shadow, mounted and rode the horse without further problems.

Rather than being angry, Philip went to Alexander as he dismounted and threw his arms around him. With obvious pride, he declared, "You'll have to find another kingdom; Macedonia is not large enough for you." It is a good example of Plutarch's dictum about the importance of small things in revealing character, both Philip's and Alexander's. It also rings true because of its Macedonian context. Alexander had been taught to ride from an early age, as had most Macedonian noble youths, so his expertise would be normal. Alexander named the horse Bucephalus (Oxhead) for his most prominent feature and rode the horse until it died on campaign in India years later.

A few years after this, Philip decided to pick a teacher for Alexander's more mature schooling. A competition was held for this honor and announced throughout Greece. Philip's choice fell to one of his own boyhood friends who was the son of Nicomachus, the court physician to Philip's father, Amyntas III. That man was Aristotle. In him, Philip found not only the brightest intellectual light of the age, or arguably any age, but someone who knew Macedonia well and what was expected from an Argead prince.

Aristotle came to Macedonia in 343 B.C.E., but not just to tutor Alexander. A school for all the royal pages (*basilokoi paides*) was established at the Nymphaeion at Mieza, near modern Naoussa. The pages were the sons of the important families of Macedonia, maintained at the king's expense. They acted as squires and attendants to the king and his court, while also serving as pledges for the good behavior of their families. They were the future Companions of the King. By this point, Demosthenes of Athens had been taunting Philip in his speeches, calling him a barbarian with rude habits. Aristotle was to teach all of them and remove any future stigma Demosthenes might cast on Macedonia and her court. Secondarily, the school was established to get the students out of Pella and away from court, and more directly, to get Alexander away from Olympias' influence.

For the next three years, the youths were taught the traditional Greek concepts of excellence (arete) and virtue. In Homeric terms, this was "to be the best." Alexander was particularly open to Homeric training, since he felt most akin to Achilles. Aristotle wrote out a special copy of the *Iliad* for Alexander, which he kept under his pillow throughout his campaigns, along with a dagger, equally the mark of an Argead prince.

The course of study included mathematics, natural philosophy (science), and medicine, for which Alexander and Ptolemy, the future king of Egypt, had a passion; ethics and philosophy, for which other students, especially Seleucus, the future king of Syria, had an aptitude; and the poetry of Hesiod, Pindar, and Homer, for which Cassander, the future king of Macedonia, was most noted. Aristotle also wrote two treatises for Alexander especially: *On Colonizing* and *Concerning Kingship*. Later, Alexander showed he had taken those lessons to heart.

Leonidas continued as Alexander's moral exemplar. Once while offering a sacrifice, Alexander used two handfuls of incense (literally worth more than their weight in gold) as a sacrifice on the burning brazier before the gods. He was scolded by Leonidas for being wasteful. Years later, when Alexander took Gaza, the main shipping point for incense imported from southern

Arabia, he sent Leonidas 18 tons of the precious substance, demonstrating that he had not learned the lesson. Generosity and the extravagant gesture were always to be hallmarks of Alexander's character.

Athletic competition was a regular part of Greek education and training, for both mental and physical conditioning. Alexander developed a fondness for this sort of contest and would frequently hold games for the army to celebrate and break the monotony of the march. His friends even suggested that Alexander enter the *stadion*, the 200-meter race which was the primary event in the Olympic Games, and from which our term "stadium" is derived. Alexander said he would do so if all his fellow competitors were kings. His attitude was strictly Homeric: that such games were an aristocratic preserve designed to demonstrate excellence. The Olympic Games were already plagued with professional athletes, and this was Alexander's way of making a statement. Again confidence and spirit were foremost, and he would soon need those.

Alexander's training at Mieza continued for three years. Then in 340 B.C.E., he entered a new phase and left Mieza to assume genuine political responsibilities under his father's most trusted friend, Antipater. Philip's campaigns had necessitated his frequent absence from Pella. On those occasions, the affairs of the kingdom were invariably left under the direction of Antipater. Interesting in his own right, Antipater had been a general under Perdikkas and was a close friend and correspondent of Aristotle and the author of a history of Macedonia's Illyrian wars. More importantly in this context, he was acknowledged as the most loyal and trusted man in the kingdom. Alexander was now sixteen years old, and Antipater was to begin his tutelage in political affairs, to teach Alexander how to rule a kingdom.

Philip's relations with the Greeks and his expansion eastward further into Thrace had now reached a critical stage. In 340 B.C.E., Philip began by campaigning in the Bosporus against Byzantium and Perinthus, openly opposed by Athens. Alexander was named as regent for the kingdom in Philip's absence, with Antipater as his adviser. But it was more than politics. In campaigning at the far eastern end of the northern Aegean, Philip was exposing a long left flank to possible interference. During the summer, both Antipater and Parmenio campaigned independently against northern tribes in the area of the Tetrachoritai. As part of that campaign, Alexander operated against a tribe called the Maedi, defeated them and founded a city in their territory which he called Alexandropolis, "the city of Alexander," after himself.

This incident has frequently been wrongly characterized as an example of Alexander's arrogance, ambition, and hotheadedness. It was, in fact, part of a carefully orchestrated set of operations. The willfulness was in the name Alexander chose for the city, not the campaign. Naming a city after yourself was a royal prerogative, one which was not yet Alexander's right to excercise, and Philip chided him for it, suggesting he wait to do such things until Philip was dead and Alexander *was* king. But Philip let the name stand, demonstrating again the philosophy that you can teach discipline to the bold, and that his purpose was to nurture and not break Alexander's spirit. There is one other point for future reference. The population settled into Alexandropolis was a mixed one ethnically (Macedonian and local) and intended to create a Macedonian center to stabilize their presence in the region while at the same time incorporate the local population. It is a technique Alexander would use later to good effect in Asia.

Now Philip took Alexander directly under his wing. The break with Athens was open, and an alliance was forming against Macedon. Philip had no intention of turning south until the north was secure and spent 339 B.C.E. campaigning up the Hebrus River into the central Balkans to prevent Athens from stirring up those Thracian tribes in his absence, a tactic Athens had used for more than a century. Alexander accompanied Philip, learning the king's concepts of command, strategy, and tactics. The fighting was fierce at times, and Philip was wounded in the thigh by a blow so severe it killed the horse he was riding. By the end of the year, Alexander had proven himself to Philip and been placed in command of the Companion Cavalry.

But the final lesson in war came at Chaeronea the next year. It was Alexander's charge that rolled up the Greek allied line and, as noted, the Macedonians voted him the hero of the battle. He had learned the lessons. This was followed by Alexander's mission to Athens, again with Antipater as his adviser. By this point Alexander's appetite for royal power was growing, fed both by Olympias' own ambitions and by Philip's triumphal progress through Greece. Philip's designs for Greece and the east, to which he had always been drawn, were rapidly developing; the war with Persia was imminent. Philip was clearly the central figure of his times, and Alexander began to become jealous of that position and his own secondary role in those plans.

Alexander and the Death of Philip

The summer of 337 B.C.E. brought a number of disappointments to Alexander. As the League of

Corinth took shape, Alexander told his friends, ". . . and for me, [Philip] will leave no great or shining achievement to show to the World." Dynastic politics were further complicated when Philip married again, for the first time to a Macedonian. It was a love match with a young girl named Cleopatra (a common name for Macedonian girls) from an up-country noble family. She was the niece of Attalus, the general later sent by Philip along with Parmenio to seize a bridgehead in Asia Minor and prepare for Philip's invasion.

Older scholarship has suggested that this marriage was an insult to Alexander's mother and turned Alexander against Philip. If so, it was a little late in the day, as Philip had married five times since Alexander's birth. The truth probably lies in the possibility of another heir being born, this one with a Macedonian heritage, which might prove inherently more popular with the army, but regardless one that would give a counterpoint to Alexander as heir to the throne. Up to this point, Alexander's only rival among Philip's other children was Arrhidaeus, who was mentally disabled, possibly as the result of an attempted poisoning by Olympias. Even so, when Philip tried to arrange a marriage for Arrhidaeus with the daughter of Pixodarus, a Persian satrap in Asia Minor, Alexander tried to intervene and offer himself as a bridegroom instead. It was a direct challenge to Philip's authority, diplomacy, and policy. Philip's goal was to pave the way for his campaigns in Asia Minor, but Alexander could only see the personal aspect. And it didn't work. It also revealed how vulnerable in Macedonian dynastic politics Alexander felt, even though he was popular in the army. The logical reason for this behavior was that there now was the chance of a much more direct threat to that inheritance made by Philip's new bride and possible children.

That very possibility cropped up at the wedding feast itself, when all the men had stayed on to drink, including Philip. Attalus proposed a toast to the new union and the hopes that it would produce "a legitimate heir." It was a direct insult to Alexander, who was present. The young prince shouted back, "You would make a bastard of me!" and tossed a goblet of wine in Attalus' face. Not surprisingly, a fight broke out between them, and when Philip moved to separate them he tripped and fell flat on his face. Alexander sneered, "Behold Philip, who would conquer Asia but cannot cross from one couch to another!"

The emotions and feelings behind this exchange can only be guessed at, and modern values and psychology are not much help in analyzing things 2300 years past and in a very different society.

The truth behind it was that Alexander had been pushing things, clearly talking and acting disloyally if not treasonably. It could also partially be the result of Olympias' stories about Alexander's divine birth backfiring on them both. In any event, Alexander left Pella the next morning, along with his mother, rather than face a Philip both angry *and* sober. He took Olympias to her home in Epirus and he went into voluntary exile among the Agrianian tribesmen of the north.

For a year Alexander was totally out of the picture. Plans for the invasion of Persia progressed. The League of Corinth was established, with Philip named as Hegemon (Commander) of Greece. The advance force not only seized a bridgehead, but moved as far south as Ephesus, more than halfway along the coast, which they held for several weeks. In the spring of that new year, Cleopatra bore Philip a child. One ancient source states that it was a daughter named Europa, but subsequent actions may indicate that it was in fact a son. Nevertheless, through the effort of both Alexander's and Philip's friends, a reconciliation was worked out. The child was a newborn, and Alexander was still the only viable heir.

Early that summer of 336 B.C.E., Philip officiated at the marriage of Alexander's sister, who was also named Cleopatra, to his uncle, the Hegemon of the Epirote League, whose name

also was Alexander. It was the occasion for the
return of Philip's son, and in all probability
Olympias, to Pella. Uncle/niece marriages were
not uncommon in dynastic situations in antiquity, and Philip had recently put the Epirote
Alexander on the throne of the Molossi, which
made him Commander of the League. This marriage alliance would cement that relationship.
Philip's plans called for this Alexander to lead
a force west into the Greek area of Italy in order
to bring the Greek cities there into the League
of Corinth, thereby establishing a Hellenic
Oikumene, a Greek world community.

Following the marriage at Aegae, Philip held a
procession to honor the Olympic Pantheon of
Gods, during which the images of the twelve major deities were to be carried into the theater, immediately followed by Philip himself. It was a
propaganda ploy, with Philip intending to number himself among the Olympians. After the
event, much like the death of Caesar and the Ides
of March, a number of foreboding omens were
recalled including a Delphic Oracle's prediction.
Regardless of whatever truth there may be in the
existence of these rumors, Philip had been persuaded as a gesture of good faith to let his bodyguards draw away from him. He was escorted
only by the two Alexanders (his son and son-in-
law), several paces behind him. At this point

Philip was struck down from his blind side by one of his own bodyguards, one Pausanias.

After the blow was struck, Pausanias ran to a group of horses tethered near the edge of the theater but was pursued by a number of Alexander's friends and cut down, without offering resistance. Much as in the assassination of John F. Kennedy, both in antiquity and among modern scholars, theories about true motivations and conspiracies abounded. These theories ranged from Pausanias acting alone, based on a personal grudge actually held against the general Attalus, but one that Philip refused to rectify, to a full-blown conspiracy involving Olympias and Alexander. There were a number of factors that fed this theory: that Pausanias was conveniently killed and therefore could not be questioned; that the assassin's death was due to friends of Alexander; and that Pausanias offered no resistance, possibly because he thought of his killers as fellow conspirators, which was compounded by the fact he was running to a group of horses (not just one) in order to make his escape.

Plutarch recounts that it was Olympias who fanned Pausanias' grudge into rage and turned him against Philip. He also includes a story about Alexander egging Pausanias on by taunting him with a line from one of Euripides' plays. And Justin likewise encourages this view, but both of these stories come from sources written more than three hundred years after the events and after the defamatory propaganda of the wars following Alexander's death. There was no proof.

Alexander was hailed as king by Alexander of Lynkos. But it was Antipater and Parmenio who endorsed Alexander as king before the Macedonian army assembly that very day. Had they or the army suspected Alexander, he wouldn't have survived, given the Macedonians' devotion to Philip. Alexander did state that it was a conspiracy and implicated (conveniently) possible rivals to the throne, such as his cousin Amyntas. An unlikely prospect was the general Attalus, who nevertheless was killed in Asia Minor at the bridgehead, allegedly for conspiring with Athens after the event. And oddly, Alexander of Lynkos' older brothers were named. Later Alexander of Lynkos, too, would be executed for complicity in "the plot" but also tied to conspiring with the Persians. These deaths cemented Alexander's position and gave the phalanx at least the sense of revenge for Philip's loss.

The act of burial of a king is in itself a royal act establishing the authority of the successor, and Alexander conducted the funeral rites for his father at Aegae, the modern village of Vergina. A tomb complex has in fact been excavated there containing three *tumuli* (large mounds) covering chambered burials, which in turn were covered by a giant *tumulus*. The remains are undoubtedly the last members of the Argead house buried at Aegea, though there is considerable debate as to which family members are buried there. Logically, they are Philip II, Philip III, Arrhidaeus, Alexander's half-brother, as well as his wife, Eurydice, and Alexander IV, Alexander the Great's son. The material remains from Tombs II and III, which were found intact, are remarkable, and if Tomb II is that of Philip III, it probably contains artifacts from Alexander's reign and campaigns.

As is normal in such events, however much Alexander tried to maintain a sense of continuity, another sense of disquiet lurked below the surface in Macedonia. There was the possibility that Pausanias was actually in Persian pay, presuming that this would preempt the invasion, a charge that Alexander later accepted. To Alexander this was not a contradiction to the original plot as he knew it, but an elaboration, albeit a convenient one in regard to the Persians. Further, Olympias' subsequent actions kept things stirred up. Pausanias' body had been crucified over Philip's grave, but she crowned it with a golden wreath. In Alexander's absence later that summer, Olympias also killed Philip's child by Cleopatra and forced Cleopatra to kill herself, settling up an old score. Antipater may have suspected Olympias equally of a role in Philip's death, and a strong enmity developed between them. But Alexander, aged twenty, was now king of Macedonia. His first proclamation was that nothing had changed but the name of the king.

King Alexander: The First Years

Alexander's proclamation that nothing had changed was more than an attempt to calm things down in Macedonia. It was a declaration that all of his father's policies, alliances, and treaty arrangements were maintained, because it was normal for such relations to end with the death of the king who had promulgated them. But the news of Philip's death was received joyously in Athens, and a golden crown was voted the assassin, meaningless since he could not claim it, but an attempt to make political capital out of the act. Demosthenes stated that Athena and Zeus had foretold the event to him, and he walked about garlanded with flowers.

More importantly, Demosthenes immediately began to negotiate a new anti-Macedonian coalition including Thebes and the Thessalian League. The Thessalians tried to block the Vale of Tempe, the main pass around Mount Olympus into the region, but Alexander showed he had learned his father's lessons well. Quick movement was the key, and he had steps cut across

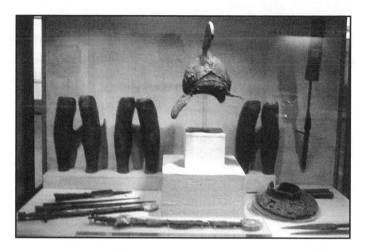

Collection of artifacts from Tomb II at Vergina, including a helmet, pectoral (throat protector), greaves (shin guards), sarissa spear points and spiked counterweights, sword, and a torch. (Photograph by Winthrop Lindsay Adams, taken at the Archaeological Museum at Thessaloniki.)

the side of Mount Ossa to bypass the Vale and brought the full Macedonian army into Thessaly. The Thessalian League responded by electing him Tagos (war-leader) and Archon (administrator) of Thessaly for life: a bloodless victory. At the same time, the Delphic Amphictyony confirmed Alexander as hegemon of Greece and awarded Alexander the votes in the Council which had previously been Philip's.

The army continued on to Thebes and pitched camp outside the city. Thebes officially renewed the alliance with Macedonia. While the army was still there, an embassy was sent from Athens to apologize for their actions. Alexander continued his own triumphal progress on to Corinth, where the League of Corinth reconfirmed the alliance which was to invade Persia. Within a matter of weeks, without any bloodshed, Alexander had reasserted his father's control of affairs and assumed his position in Greece.

It must have been an exhilarating moment, and while in Corinth, Alexander and his friends strode about to see the sites and people. Among these was the philosopher Diogenes of Sinope. Diogenes' philosophy was to live a life of asceticism, rejecting the material world. He lived in a broken jar in the marketplace and got the nickname "Kynikos" (doglike), which was later applied to his philosophical school, the Cynics. Alexander came upon Diogenes sunning himself. As Alexander's shadow fell across Diogenes, so the story goes, Alexander rather grandly asked what he could do for Diogenes. The reply was that Alexander could stop blocking his sunlight. Alexander told his Companions that if he were not Alexander, "I would be Diogenes." Legend was already growing around him.

On the return trip, Alexander swung through Delphi to receive a pronouncement on his reign from the Oracle of Apollo. The Pythoness, the priestess who gave the oracles, did so only at prescribed times of the month, and Alexander had already missed those. Not to be denied, Alexander dragged her by the hand toward the Oracle, during the course of which she said, "Lad, you are unconquerable (*Aniketos*)!" That was enough of an omen for him, and Alexander let her go. He was beginning to acquire, by one means or another, the trappings of a reputation and an image carefully crafted to overawe. He already had adopted a motto for his reign from the *Iliad*. This was Helen's description of the king of Mycenae, and a Greek hegemon like himself, Agamemnon: "Both a good king and a strong spear fighter." Again, the identification obviously reinforced Alexander's position and image.

If the remainder of the year 336 B.C.E. was spent with a certain amount of political posturing, the next year was spent proving that Alexander was the real thing and no shadow king. In order to season the army under his command, Alexander campaigned as his father had done up into the central Balkans. This served a number of purposes. First, it was necessary to conduct some demonstrations among the northern barbarian tribes to make sure they remained quiet when he later invaded Asia Minor, the same reason Philip had done so before Chaeronea. These tribes, going back some 200 years, had traditionally allied with Persia, and latterly Athens, and Alexander needed a secure area left behind him. Second, Alexander had placed some of his own friends and companions in key command positions and they needed experience in those posts. Parmenio's sons, Philotas and Nicanor, were appointed to command the Companion Cavalry (Hetairoi) and the Guards Brigade (Hypaspists) respectively, while Kleitos the Black now commanded the Agema, Alexander's personal cavalry guard and the unit with which he preferred to fight. Other appointments had been made to the territorial brigades. Finally, the army itself had to be given confidence in both Alexander and his new officers.

Alexander moved to Philippi as his staging area and then on to the Kajan Pass to attack the Triballi, who held the heights and the passage into the upper Balkans. It was a daunting task to attack uphill against fierce tribesmen, who had the added advantage of carts filled with rocks to roll down on the assault force, intending to break up the attack. With Alexander himself in the lead, he ordered forward the Guards and the Agrianian mercenary javelin men, a relic of his time in exile with that tribe. He told the assault team that when he gave the orders, they were to throw themselves flat on the ground, with their shields above them. When the Triballi shoved the carts over the top to plummet downhill onto his men, Alexander gave the word. His troops did as ordered and the carts rumbled harmlessly over them. With renewed respect, they rose and took the heights, killing 3000 of the Triballi without a single loss to themselves.

Alexander decided to pursue the tribesmen and not let them regroup. He was also seized, as he said, by a pothos (an undeniable urge) to see the Danube River (the ancient Ister), one of the legendary boundaries of the civilized world. There the Triballi had joined up with a Celtic tribe, the Getae, on the northern bank of the river. While his army made obvious preparations to cross the river in the face of the enemy, Alexander actually slipped west, upstream, with 4000 infantry and 1500 cavalry. They crossed at night. As the allied tribesmen stood facing the Macedonian army across the river on the south bank, to their right they heard an odd swishing sound. Suddenly Alexander and his men emerged from the fields, leveling the high grass with their spears. Completely surprised, the tribes fled, abandoning their families, camp, and possessions. Alexander had won another bloodless victory.

In order to get their families and possessions back, the Getae and Triballi came to terms. They promised not to attack Alexander's lands and possessions; and should they break their oath, they called on the sea to rise and drown them,

the earth to open to swallow them, or the sky to
fall on them. The Celtic Getae mentioned that
they really only feared the last of these, an interesting bit of folklore as it is the first recounting
of the later Celtic Irish fable of "Henny Penny"
and the sky falling.

Word now reached Alexander that a revolt
had broken out in Illyria around the town of
Pelium, led by a chieftain named Kleitos (not to
be confused with Alexander's cavalry commander
of the same name). Alexander moved immediately to the city and besieged it. When Illyrian
forces came up to relieve the siege, Alexander
got rid of them and stopped the further spread of
the rebellion by simply putting the Macedonian
phalanx through a series of complicated battlefield maneuvers in dead silence. It was all the
proof the Illyrians needed that they were out-
matched, and it was another bloodless victory
for Alexander. Few thing impress soldiers more
than success without casualties, and Alexander's
stock among his Macedonians rose immeasurably.

He still had Kleitos to deal with, and the Illyrian chieftain was staying put. Alexander couldn't
afford to be pinned down in a long siege, nor to let
Kleitos off. As a ruse, Alexander faked a retreat,
much as his father had at Chaeronea, to draw
Kleitos out. Then, using catapults as field artillery to clear the far bank, he forced a crossing

of the Eordaicus River. Confronted in the open, Kleitos surrendered, again without any loss to the Macedonians.

By this time, Alexander had been away in the central, northern, and western Balkans all summer. A rumor of his death, based on no more than wishful thinking, began to circulate in Greece at this point, fanned by Demosthenes in the further hope of putting together another anti-Macedonian alliance. In Thebes, two Macedonian officers were caught unawares and murdered by a Theban mob. The Macedonian garrison in the Theban citadel, called the Cadmeia, was besieged. Thebes was in open opposition. This news now reached Alexander at Pelium.

The seriousness of the situation was obvious to Alexander. The sooner he reacted, the less the chance there was of this spreading to the other Greek states. In the fourth campaign of that summer, without pausing, Alexander moved quickly. In seven days he was in Thessaly, the army having covered 35 miles a day in some of the roughest terrain in existence. Here he was met by Antipater with the rest of the Macedonian army, siege equipment, engineers, and fresh supplies. Six days later, the full Macedonian levy was approaching Thebes, even before word that Alexander was still alive had reached them. The next day Alexander camped before Thebes itself.

Alexander gave the Thebans three days to ask for terms, while Greek allies from the surrounding areas flocked to Alexander's standard. On the fourth day, he attacked. The problem was similar to that in Pelium; he had to end this quickly, before Demosthenes could put together an alliance, and a long, drawn-out siege was out of the question. Alexander decided to use a variant of the same tactics he had used against Kleitos: draw the Thebans out. One territorial brigade, seemingly on its own, attacked the main gate at Thebes. Seeing an opportunity to sting the Macedonians, the Thebans drove it back, opening the gates to drive them fully from the approaches to the city. Suddenly the remaining brigades of the phalanx, which had been hidden from view, attacked, and one group dashed ahead to intermingle with the Thebans and make it impossible for the defenders to close the gates. The goal was to seize the gates and hold them for the rest of the army. It succeeded, and the Macedonian garrison broke out of the Cadmeia at the same time. Thebes fell on the first day of the assault. It had been eighteen days since Alexander had heard of original events at Thebes. Rapid deployment was to be a hallmark of all of Alexander's campaigns.

As they broke into the city, the Greek allies began to butcher the Theban civilian population.

These allies were mostly from neighboring cities who had suffered under the Theban domination of the region for centuries. Theban actions had included wiping whole cities out on occasion, and this was the Greeks' revenge. Some 6000 were killed before Alexander—not the Greeks—could bring it to an end. It was the Macedonian army which ended the slaughter.

The question now was what to do. Thebes had broken both its own alliance with Macedonia and its oath when joining the League of Corinth. Alexander left the decision to the Greek allies, presumably to the League of Corinth itself. The League voted to carry out what the Greeks called an andropodysmos, a "breaking of the people" in which every man and boy over thirteen years of age was killed, the women and children were sold into slavery, and the city was razed to the ground. It is precisely what Thebes had done twice to Orchomenos, its rival in Boeotia, and once to Plataea, its neighbor. To his credit (and he is rarely given credit for this), Alexander did not carry out the killings. But the population, some 30,000, were sold into slavery and the city destroyed, except for the temples and the house of the poet Pindar.

No decision of the allies could be made without Alexander's approval, and he has frequently been condemned both in antiquity and modern times for these actions. It was a matter of policy. Alexander was about to embark on a campaign in Asia Minor, and traditional Persian policy when faced by a strong Greek force (whether Athenian, or Spartan, or whomever) had been to stir up trouble in Greece behind them. Alexander could not afford to let that happen, so an example had to be made of Thebes. Nevertheless, it was a joint vote of the Greeks themselves that authorized it, and it was Alexander who spared the Thebans their lives. In the aftermath, Athens once again apologized and exiled Demosthenes "for counseling evil things." Now Alexander could begin preparations for attacking Persia.

The Persian Empire

Before going any further, it is necessary to take a look at the Persian Empire Alexander would face. As background to that, the history of Persia encompassed its meteoric rise from a relatively small tribal canton in the southern Zagros Mountains, east of what is now Iraq, into an empire that stretched from northwestern India (modern Pakistan) to the eastern shore of the Mediterranean Sea and from Egypt to the south central Asian republics of the former Soviet Union. In two generations, it grew to a size roughly equal to that of the United States of America, with a population of some eighty million people.

The conquests were largely accomplished by two rulers from what was called the Achaemenid dynasty: Cyrus the Great (reigned ca. 557–530 B.C.E.) and his son, Cambyses (reigned 530–522 B.C.E.). In doing so, they united virtually all of the states of the ancient Near East. The final portion, India, was added by the third ruler of the dynasty, Darius I, called "the Great" (reigned 521–487 B.C.E.). It was his organizational genius that gave the Persian empire its actual form.

Darius made clear his position in the hierarchy as Great King, "King of Kings" (Shah-in-Shah in Persian) in the Behistun Inscription, which celebrated his victory in the civil war which brought him to power. There follows that declaration about a dozen lines of royal titles: king of the Persians; king of the Medes (and then a dozen or so other Iranian tribes); king of Babylon; king of Lydia; Pharaoh of Egypt; and so on. The philosophy behind this was not merely to be grandiose. The physical identity, laws, customs, and religions of those peoples were maintained. To the average citizens of a Mesopotamian town, only the name of the ruler was changed, not their day-to-day life. A policy of religious tolerance was adopted, rather than the usual theocentric view that had been the hallmark of most eastern empires.

The empire was divided into twenty provinces, or satrapies, each ruled in the Great King's name by a Persian governor, or satrap. Within each province, the satrap had full civil, economic, and military authority. But the laws, customs, and religion of the local population were protected. The empire was bound together by several megahighways running from Sardis in Asia Minor (in the northwest) and Memphis in Egypt (in the southwest) to Babylon. From Babylon the main highway led east to Susa (at the main pass through the Zagros Mountains), and then north to the summer capital at Ecbatana (modern Hamadan), and south to the winter capital at Persepolis. Roads from these two complexes crossed the Iranian plateau and connected to the ancient silk routes to China and spice route to India. They were built to accommodate easy troop movements but, like the interstate highway system in the United States, also made transcontinental trade easier.

Darius also created a standard unit of coinage, the gold daric, to unite the area's economy and encourage trade. Controlling these routes and the western distribution points for these commodities including silk and spice made Persia fabulously wealthy. In doing so, the peoples along the trade routes and local merchants conducting this traffic also prospered. The result was that, within the empire and for its average subject, Persian rule delivered peace, prosperity, religious freedom, and the protection of your own laws. It was the Persians who ended the Babylonian captivity and endorsed the return to Judaea for the Hebrews. They even sponsored the rebuilding of the Second Temple in Jerusalem. All these actions were demonstrative of a Persian policy that lasted for the duration of Darius' reign but began to deteriorate after that in terms of religious tolerance.

To protect this area from outside pressure and secure it from within, Cyrus created a large army on the Near Eastern model. Darius inherited and perfected it. Soldiers were organized into squads of ten, companies of one hundred, regiments of one thousand, and divisions of 10,000 according to their type of armament. That meant units of archers, light infantry (javelinmen), heavy infantry (spearmen), horse archers, lancers, and so forth. These units were formed from each ethnic group. Persians, Medes, and other Iranians made up the backbone of the army, but each of the subject peoples also served according to their own national traditions (Bedouin camel corps, Indian elephant squadrons, Egyptian infantry). The Greeks from Asia Minor normally provided sailors and rowers for the Persian Navy. Combined units of the army were assigned to each governor, both to protect the province and to maintain peace and order.

This mixed recruiting and type of service fulfilled two functions. First, it meant the Persians could field huge armies. The contemporary Greek accounts for these numbers are fantastic and unreliable, running into the many hundreds of thousands. But one must keep perspective. For the average Greek city which could field a phalanx of 800 men, the difference between a million men and one hundred thousand is not arithmetic; it is simply more soldiers than they could even contemplate. Second, by having all of the peoples of the empire represented in such a Grand Army, the Persians also had hostages for the good behavior of their subjects back home.

And that was the problem. Despite the benefits of Persian rule, there were peoples of ancient traditions who preferred their independence. Among them were the Greeks.

Persia and the Greeks

Contact between the Persians and the Greeks went back more than two hundred years before Alexander. In conquering Asia Minor, Cyrus the Great had brought the Greeks living along the western coast under imperial control. In normal times, they had been permitted local autonomy; they became wealthy because they were the western termini and shipping points for many of the trade goods from the East; and they served in the Persian Navy.

But under Darius the area had rebelled, freedom and autonomy being uppermost in the Greek mind. Following the suppression of this Ionian Revolt (named for the main Greek coastal area in Asia Minor), Darius' policy had determined that in order to keep control of the Asian Greeks, Persia should conquer the remaining Greeks in the Aegean basin and Greek mainland. The Ionians had received aid from the Greek homeland in their revolt. To Darius it was simply rounding off the empire, just as he had done in conquering the Indus Valley (modern Pakistan).

It was precisely here that the Persian juggernaut came to a halt. In two invasion attempts, the second culminating in the Greek victory at Marathon, Darius failed utterly. In a third attempt, Darius' son, Xerxes (reigned 487–465 B.C.E.), was defeated and an army of 80,000 crushed in 479 B.C.E. at Plataea in central Greece. What followed was the rise of the Athenian empire, which freed the Asian Greeks from Persian control. But in the massive struggle between Athens and Sparta at the end of the fifth century, a Greek civil war had begun. It was Persian gold which made possible a Spartan victory in the Peloponnesian War.

The Persian who had coordinated that aid to Sparta was Cyrus, the younger son of Darius II (reigned 424–404 B.C.E.). He had established firm friendships among the Spartan commanders and knew the value of Greek heavy (phalanx) infantry. The Persian price for their aid was to be (at least) the collection of tribute from the Asia Minor Greeks, and Persia had never given up its claims on the region. Following the death of his father, and a brief imprisonment, Cyrus made an attempt to overthrow his older brother, Artaxerxes II (reigned 404–358 B.C.E.). In doing so he enlisted some 10,000 Greek mercenaries as the key to his army and marched them along the great highway from Sardis in Asia Minor toward Babylon. At a place called Cunaxa, just above Babylon, he met Artaxerxes in battle and the Greek mercenaries broke through the Persian army easily. However, Cyrus was killed in a cavalry skirmish at the end of the battle. The Greeks had won the day, but lost the war.

Artaxerxes, in a ruse to end this Greek threat, offered to take the mercenaries into his own service. He killed their officers at a banquet, presuming that the mercenaries would break up and could be killed piecemeal. The Greeks merely elected new officers, including the Athenian Xenophon, who later wrote up the whole adventure in a work called the *Anabasis* or "the March Up Country." From the heart of the Persian empire, those 10,000 Greeks cut their way out to Trapezus on the Black Sea coast, and from there back to the Aegean. It was a point not lost on Artaxerxes. If so small a number of Greeks could not be stopped, what would a large, well-organized force be able to accomplish?

With the death of Cyrus the Younger, all ties were broken with Sparta and hostilities broke out between the Greeks and Persians again. During the course of that war, Persian policy began to crystalize. Knowing that there were many Greek states discontented with the Spartan domination that had supplanted Athens, Artaxerxes began supplying gold to them. It was a continuation of the policy which brought an end to the Peloponnesian War, but its purpose now was to continue a Greek civil war rather than end it. By pouring gold into one side or another, Persia could maintain a balance of terror in Greece, and keep them at one another's throats. That kept the Greeks out of Persian affairs and weak. By 387 B.C.E., Greece was exhausted and asked the Great King to broker a peace (usually called the King's Peace, as a result). The first step was to cede the Asian Greeks back to Persian control. A Common Peace was declared and all alliances were broken up. Persian gold had bought what Persian arms had failed to win, at least the passive control of Greece and the safety of Asia Minor.

As a byproduct, after more than a century of almost continuous warfare in Greece, there were many who earned their living as soldiers. The mercenaries employed by Cyrus the Younger had been an example of this. Those men were now available to enter Persian service, where they were needed to suppress internal revolts that were becoming endemic elsewhere in the empire, as we shall see. One might well ask why Persia didn't develop her own heavy-armed phalanx. The creation of such an army relies on an independent middle class, willing to submit freely to the kind of discipline necessary to fight on that level. Soldiers who do so invariably want a say in such a government. The history of Greece, and Rome for that matter, is the story of its citizen soldiers. The great king was unwilling to introduce this as a permanent aspect of his government and empower his own middle class, especially since it was far easier for him to rent such soldiers for as long as he needed and keep control himself.

Fourth–Century Persia

The history of Persia from the close of the Cyrus' Cunaxa campaign down to Alexander's invasion is largely of one piece: rebellious provinces, satraps seeking to become independent, and weak monarchs. Cyrus' rebellion against Artaxerxes II merely set the stage. Egypt was independent from 404 B.C.E. on, under a new native line of

Pharaohs (XXVIII Dynasty) led by one Amyrtaeus.

From Egypt, as each attempt to reconquer it failed, rebellion would spread to the Levant (Israel and Lebanon), Cyprus, and Asia Minor. The Great King would spend a decade or so suppressing these rebellions at the western fringe of the Empire. Then another attempt would be made to reconquer Egypt. It was a debilitating process, which saw Darius the Great's old conquests in the Hindu Kush and the Sind, the valley of the Indus, likewise break away. The empire was disintegrating, but Egypt was the major obsession. Greece was only a potential danger, which the policy of the King's Peace seemed to handle: playing the Greeks off against one another.

Artaxerxes was concerned with reasserting his authority in Asia Minor and Cyprus first. The satrap Datames brought Asia Minor under control in the mid-380's B.C.E. The coalition of rebellious cities on Cyprus, led by Evagoras, the Greek King of Salamis, were defeated at sea in 381 B.C.E. and came to terms. This cleared the way for an invasion of Egypt. Command for this was initially given to Datames, but he was relieved of it before the expedition set out because Artaxerxes was jealous of his success.

For most of the period Artaxerxes stayed in Susa or Persepolis, where he quickly fell under the influence of his harem and court politics. Artaxerxes was indolent and cruel by nature, and it was as fatal to succeed under him as it was to fail. He earned the nickname "Mnemon" (the Rememberer), because he never forgot any slight or insult to himself.

The Egyptian expedition finally set out in 374 B.C.E. under the general Pharnabazus, but he quarrelled with his Greek mercenary commander, the Athenian Iphicrates. The expedition failed, and in the wake of that failure a satraps' revolt broke out. First Datames seized Sinope on the Asia Minor Black Sea coast and ruled it as if he were an independent monarch. By 366 B.C.E. Ariobarzanes broke Phrygia (in central Asia Minor) away as well. Then the satrap Orontes led Armenia out of the empire. The whole Mediterranean and Aegean coasts, Greek and Phoenician, rose in rebellion.

In this the rebels were supported by the new Egyptian Pharaoh Nectanebo, and later by his son, Tachos. In turn, Egypt received a good deal of aid from Greece. Greek mercenaries filled Egypt's armies and in this period they were commanded by no less a person than the Spartan King Agesilaus. Chabrias of Athens commanded the Egyptian fleet.

In the long run, the satraps distrusted one another more than they feared Artaxerxes, which was a big mistake. Though the revolt continued to 359 B.C.E., the year Philip II came to the throne of Macedon, one by one the rebels were dealt with. Orontes went over to the king in exchange for recognition of his authority in Armenia. Datames was assassinated. Ariobarzanes was betrayed and crucified. By 359 B.C.E., the rest had come over on the same terms as Orontes, reappointment to their satrapies. Artaxerxes died during the winter of 359–358 B.C.E., in control of everything except Egypt.

His successor was Artaxerxes III Ochus (reigned 358–338 B.C.E.), whose first act was to kill off his numerous brothers and half-brothers. In 356 B.C.E., he ordered the satraps to disband their provincial armies on the grounds that those who did were no threat, and those who didn't would rebel anyway. Only two did not: Artabazus of Phrygia and Orontes of Armenia. The former wound up fleeing to Philip's court in Macedonia, to be questioned by Alexander; Orontes came to terms.

Now Artaxerxes Ochus planned to attack Egypt, probably in 351 B.C.E., along the dangerous coast road across the Sinai Peninsula. The Great King was personally in command, but part of the army was lost in the marshes and the rest was driven back by the new Greek mercenary commander of Egypt's army, Mentor of Rhodes.

It signalled the renewal of rebellions for Armenia, Phoenicia, and Cyprus. Mentor went to garrison the Phoenician town of Sidon, as a bastion against future Persian invasion plans.

The Great King now had the same task as his father. Orontes was forced back in Armenia. A Persian fleet and army, with the aid of the Athenian mercenary naval commander Phocion and 8000 Greeks, reduced Salamis on Cyprus. Sidon was besieged by the Great King himself in 348 B.C.E. By 345 B.C.E., the city capitulated: Its beauties went to fill Artaxerxes Ochus' already well-stocked harem. Wiser than his father, however, Artaxerxes Ochus decided to employ Mentor of Rhodes and his mercenaries rather than kill them.

By 343 B.C.E., as Aristotle arrived in Macedonia to tutor the young Alexander, Artaxerxes Ochus was again ready to attack Egypt, where Nectanebo II was now Pharaoh. He gathered 10,000 Greek volunteers as well as 12,000 hardened mercenaries under Mentor of Rhodes. The Great King gave Mentor a free hand. The crafty mercenary began to buy off Nectanebo's Greek mercenaries and spread disaffection in Egypt's forces, gold always being Persia's greatest asset.

With an untrustworthy army under him, Nectanebo retreated rather than face Mentor in a pitched battle. He withdrew first to Memphis, then up the Nile all the way to Ethiopia and into obscurity. Nectanebo simply vanished into the mists of history. By 342 B.C.E., the Persians controlled the west and Mentor was set up as the satrap of the whole western area. The other power that emerged with the victory over Egypt was Bagoas, the chiliarch (or commander) of the elite 1000 men of the Great King's Palace Guard; for all intents and purposes, he was Artaxerxes Ochus' prime minister.

Mentor died in 338 B.C.E., under unknown circumstances, and his brother Memnon succeeded to the command of the Greek mercenaries, but not as satrap. In that same year, Bagoas poisoned Artaxerxes Ochus and put the young prince Arses on the throne. Two years later, Bagoas poisoned Arses as well and put his cousin Darius III Codomannus (reigned 336–330 B.C.E.) in his place. No fool in court politics, Darius promptly poisoned Bagoas, the only wise move of his reign.

Thus, Darius III came to the throne of Persia in the same year that Alexander III succeeded Philip in Macedonia, 336 B.C.E. Darius spent two years fighting rebellious satraps, who took the occasion of a regime change to try to break free. The Persians knew of Philip's and now Alexander's plans, but Darius left the initial planning for the war against Alexander to the six satraps of Asia Minor, the presumed theater of operations, and to Memnon of Rhodes, who had been an exile in Macedonia for a time and knew well the Macedonian weaknesses.

Alexander's Preparations

Planning for the grand expedition, set for the spring of 334 B.C.E., was by now already well under way. Alexander named Antipater to be regent of Macedonia and general for Europe in his absence, relying on Antipater much as Philip had before him. Additionally, four territorial infantry brigades of 1500 men each, all drawn from the lowland cantons, which were the most trustworthy, and four reinforced cavalry sqaudrons of 400 men each were left under Antipater's command to maintain order and defend the kingdom.

The expeditionary force itself consisted of six Macedonian territorial infantry brigades of 1500 men each (for a total of 9000), all drawn from the upland cantons. There was also the Guards Brigade (the Hypaspists) under command of Parmenio's son, Nicanor: three regiments of 1000 men each. This gave Alexander a force of 12,000 Macedonian phalangites (heavy infantrymen). These were matched by 12,000 Greek allied phalangites from the League of Corinth. Altogether, Alexander had 24,000 heavy infantrymen. This was supplemented by some 8000 light armed troops: Cretan archers, Agrianian javelinmen, and peltasts (light infantry).

The cavalry included 1700 men in the Hetairoi, the Companion Cavalry, under the command of Parmenio's eldest son, Philotas. The 300-man Agema (King's Own) squadron was commanded by Kleitos the Black, the brother of Alexander's old nurse. In addition, there were six Macedonian territorial cavalry squadrons, somewhat under-strength at 1400, some 400 men having been transferred to Antipater. Additionally, there were 1600 Thessalians and 500 Greek allied cavalry, bringing the total to 5200 heavy cavalry. To these were added 900 Thracian scouts, as light cavalry. The total military compliment then came to 38,100 men according to Diodorus Siculus, the only source we have on the makeup of the army.

Parmenio was to head the staff and act as second in command to Alexander. A Greek, Eumenes of Cardia, was in charge of the secretariat to keep track of orders and correspondence and maintain an official journal, the *Ephemerides* or Day Book. There was a medical as well as an engineering staff, the latter under a Greek named Diocles. Geographers, scientists, map makers (bematists), and botanists accompanied the army to send reports back to Aristotle. There was even a propaganda section under

Aristotle's nephew, Callisthenes, to write an official history and send reports of Alexander's achievements back to Greece. Nothing was omitted. It was to be the Great Expedition from the very start.

One more thing to note, however, is Alexander's attitude. There are clear indications that he was already thinking on a grander scale than Philip. While his uncle, Alexander of Epirus, would lead an army to the Greek portion of southern Italy as Philip had planned, there was no indication that Philip had thought beyond taking Asia Minor. Alexander was already thinking of a world stage. He had shown that in his despairing remark that Philip would leave him "no great or shining achievement to show the World." Equally, Alexander's *pothos* to see the Danube because it marked the edge of the civilized world demonstrated that he was thinking in those terms. He was open to these ideas; victory in Asia Minor would be only a beginning. As a counterpoint to this, he was not thinking in practical terms. Antipater and Parmenio wisely urged him to marry and beget an heir for the good of the kingdom before the expedition set out; but Alexander was not interested in this; his eyes were already on a wider world.

I I I

The Campaigns for
Western Asia

Introduction

Alexander's invasion of Persian territory, in its
Greek context, was a war to avenge the Persian
attacks on Greece in the fifth century B.C.E. As
such, Alexander was the commander of the
Greek and Macedonian forces of an alliance, the
League of Corinth, and Darius' war was with
that alliance. From the Persian perspective, and
the historical one for all intents and purposes, it
was a war against Alexander. All of the Persian
strategies will see the war in that fashion, and
Alexander as the key to all operations. The
struggle was initially personified as the conflict
between two men: The Persian Great King Darius
III and Alexander III of Macedon.

The planning of countermeasures by the Persians against Alexander ran afoul from the very

beginning. Memnon of Rhodes, who had been an exile in Macedonia and knew that the Argead throne was always precarious, suggested that a scorched earth policy would be best: Evacuate the towns, burn the crops, deny Alexander supplies. Alexander needed a quick victory to shore up his position; Memnon's strategy therefore was to deny him that. Further, there were Greek states, such as Athens and Sparta, who were waiting for an opportunity to upset Macedonia's control of Greek affairs. Without initial success, Alexander would have to pull back for lack of funds and supplies, and in the wake of that the Persians could stir up trouble in Greece. Time was on Persia's side. This had, in fact, been the Persian policy for almost three generations, and it was a proven success.

The six Persian satraps of Asia Minor were led by Arsites of Hellespontine Phrygia, the area in which the invasion would take place, and Spithridates of Lydia, the main Persian satrapy in Asia Minor. Arsites refused Memnon's strategy outright and persuaded his fellow satraps against it. He reasoned that since Alexander was the heart of the coalition, it was best to face him as soon as possible, with the express intent of killing Alexander himself. This would accomplish the same end proposed by Memnon. With no Alexander, there would be no coalition. If,

Memnon argued, Alexander could not afford to lose, wasn't it better then to hand him a defeat? Further, the cities Memnon proposed to abandon and the crops he planned to burn were the satraps' responsibility and the source of their revenues. The satraps have been criticized historically for putting their own concerns first, but that is pure hindsight. It also ignores the Persian religious sensibilities in Zoroastrianism, which saw fire as sacred, not to be polluted, and agriculture as an almost holy act bringing "wise order" out of Nature's "chaos." The real problem was that in the event the strategy didn't work.

The satraps' plan was based on sound intelligence. In the course of battle, Alexander invariably preferred fighting with his Companion Cavalry, and from Memnon the satraps knew that it was the Macedonian custom that the king be in the front ranks, leading his people. The Persian resources clearly outclassed Alexander's forces. They had 30,000 infantry, which included at least 12,000 Greek mercenaries, and possibly as many as 20,000, as sources vary on this, and 20,000 cavalry. Indeed, it was for their mounted forces that the Persians were most renowned in ancient warfare. They would simply make it the duty of every Persian cavalryman to kill Alexander. It turned out to be too simple.

Asia Minor

Alexander crossed the Hellespont and landed below the town of Ilion (Bronze-Age Troy) in the spring of 334 B.C.E. For both personal and propaganda reasons this was hardly an accident. He wanted the expedition to be identified as the new Greek heroic adventure mirroring the legendary Homeric past, and his own familial identification with Achilles reinforced this. As his ship approached the shore, Alexander cast his spear into the ground, claiming all Asia as "spear won" territory. Alexander then moved on to Ilion itself, to worship in the Temple of Athena, from which he took an ancient wooden shield which tradition held had once belonged to Achilles.

The Macedonian army moved east from there, and at the Granicus River came across the Persian field army of Asia Minor. There are two stories as to Alexander's first moves at this point. The first is that he immediately went into formation for an attack, which is highly unlikely given Alexander's experience and his later practice. The second account was that he pitched camp and waited for morning, resting his men and giving himself time to gather intelligence about the Persian troop arrangement. Regardless of which source one chooses to believe each army eventually drew up on the banks of the river facing each other in the following dispositions.

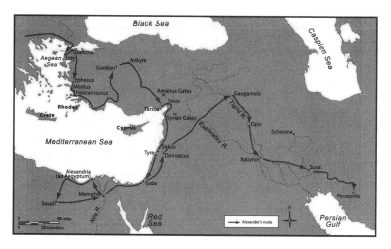

Western Asia

Alexander placed the Greek allied cavalry on the left flank, and Parmenio with the Macedonian phalanx next to them, with Parmenio commanding the whole left wing. Beside them, forming the right wing, were Nicanor and the Guards Brigade and the Macedonian Territorial and Companion Cavalry, under Alexander's personal command on the far right. The Greek infantry phalanx was held in reserve. Facing the Macedonians, the Persian cavalry was drawn up in front of their infantry, as the purpose of the battle was to overwhelm Alexander himself.

Parmenio urged caution, but Alexander opened the engagement with a cavalry charge. This was initially successful largely because it was unexpected, but it played into the Persians' strategy. The two cavalry forces were soon intertwined, and the Persian plan almost worked. Spithridates himself had fought his way to just behind Alexander and raised his sword to cut down the Macedonian king. Intent on his task at this point, Spithridates was unaware that Kleitos the Black, the commander of the Agema, was next to him, and Kleitos cut off Spithridates' arm, saving Alexander's life. Just as vitally, seeing the king in danger, Parmenion ordered the Macedonian phalanx, armed with their 18-foot sarissai, into the fight in a desperate attempt to turn the engagement. It was the Macedonian infantry which drove off the Persian cavalry and won the battle.

As the Persian cavalry fled the field, along with the light armed troops and Memnon of Rhodes, the Persian infantry, primarily the Greek mercenary force now without its commander, was left behind, entirely exposed. The Macedonians advanced to surround them. What followed was murder. Alexander refused to bargain with them, where the normal approach would have been to simply buy them out of Persian service. But all Greece (save Sparta) had taken an oath not to bear arms against Alexander, or more properly against the League of Corinth and its Hegemon, which made them criminals in Alexander's eyes.

He intended to make an example of this force as he had the city of Thebes.

The mercenaries offered fierce resistance, and the majority of Macedonian casualties were taken at this stage of the battle. Only 2000 Greek mercenaries survived, to be sent back as slaves to the mines in Macedonia. It was wasteful and foolish, for there had been nearly 60,000 Greek mercenaries in Persian pay, including several thousand Macedonians, at the beginning of the campaign. Now all of them had no option open to them but to fight to the death.

Still, it was a brilliant victory, which established Alexander as a tactical genius on the battlefield. At the loss of 25 Hetairoi and 90 infantrymen, Alexander had virtually wiped out the Persian field army in Asia Minor. Only the fleet and garrison towns remained. At least 10,000 Greek mercenaries and 6000 Persians were dead on the field. Alexander sent 300 sets of Persian arms and armor to Athens to be hung up as trophies, both to celebrate a victory that avenged the Persian burning of Athens in Xerxes' invasion and to serve as a reminder to the Greeks of where their loyalty lay. A statue was erected to commemorate the battle with the inscription that it was won by "Alexander and the Greeks except the Spartans" (equally getting in a dig against the one Greek state that had refused to join the League of Corinth).

Alexander then occupied the capital of the satrapy at Dascylion and set up a Macedonian as governor, but otherwise left the area untouched. The Persian fleet of some 400 triremes was slowly working its way north up the coast of Asia Minor, but Alexander swung inland and advanced on the main headquarters of the Persians in Asia Minor, Sardis in Lydia. Its satrap, Spithridates, lay dead at the Granicus, and the Persians withdrew, leaving both the city and the treasury. Alexander appointed another Macedonian as governor, Asander, the son of Philotas.

Rapid movement had already become a hallmark of Alexander's campaigns, and he demonstrated that now by striking west against Ephesus and covering 100 kilometers in four days. Again, the Persians simply abandoned the town and the democratic faction seized control, putting to death those oligarchs who had cooperated with the Persians. Alexander put a halt to the killing, as he had at Thebes. He issued a general amnesty and established a democratic government. A policy of leniency was emerging which would hold at least for Greek Asia Minor. It paid off, as Magnesia and Tralles followed suit and surrendered, and Alexander sent one of his officers, Alkimachus, north along the Ionian and Aeolian coast to restore autonomy to the Greek cities and establish democratic governments.

The first real resistance Alexander faced was at Miletus, the chief city of Ionia and the Persian headquarters in the district. By this point Alexander's small fleet of 160 triremes, which had been proceeding south down the Asia Minor coast, joined up and took station off the island of Lade opposite Miletus itself. This cut off the harbor at Miletus, just three days before the larger Persian fleet could come up. The Persian navy would have no effect on the outcome of the siege. After some initial skirmishing, Alexander broke through a portion of the curtain wall, while the Macedonian fleet commander, Nicanor, literally jammed his ships into the harbor. Caught between the two Macedonian forces, the city surrendered. One group of Greek mercenaries from the Persian garrison, and who thus had not been at the Granicus, escaped to an island in the harbor and prepared to fight to the last. Arrian states that "Alexander was moved to pity" by their display of loyalty and offered them terms and a place in his forces. Probably, realizing his mistake at the Granicus, Alexander's gesture was meant for propaganda purposes. If so, it was too little and too late, but a grand gesture nonetheless.

Alexander now sent Philotas, with three Territorial Infantry Brigades from the Macedonian phalanx, to seize the Persian naval base camp at Cape Mycale near Miletus, which forced the Persian fleet to withdraw from Asia Minor altogether. The Persians then took up station on the island of Samos, where the Athenian cleruchs (colonists) collaborated with them. It showed that Memnon's reasoning about Greek discontent with Alexander was not unfounded. For the time being, Alexander recognized that his small fleet was too outclassed by the Persians to be effective at sea. He paid off the crews and disbanded the fleet as too expensive to maintain. Strategically, this would later come back to haunt him as the Persian fleet, then under the command of Memnon, would seriously threaten Alexander's connections to the Greek homeland in the first half of 333 B.C.E., but for the moment he had little choice. It would be Alexander's legendary good fortune, not strategy, that would get him out of this predicament.

For now, Alexander moved on into Caria and its chief city of Halicarnassus (modern Bodrum). Caria was a frontier area, where Greek and Asian populations had mixed for centuries. It was the birthplace of Herodotus, the Greek historian of the Persian Wars. Caria had been independent under its king, Mausolus, but recently had fallen back under full Persian control, with its own Persian satrap, Orontobates. The native population welcomed Alexander, especially the rightful heir to Mausolus, Queen Ada, who was restricted to her mountain fortress at Alinda. Halicarnassus itself was occupied by the Persians and Memnon of Rhodes, who in the interim had been appointed the Persian supreme commander for Asia Minor. Memnon concentrated at Halicarnassus the mercenary garrisons which had abandoned the northern towns. Already well fortified, Memnon now strengthened the outer works of the city and hoped this would be the rock on which Alexander's campaign foundered. It almost was.

Fighting for the main town was fierce, though it is clear from Arrian's account that the Macedonians had the best of it. Still it was a siege measured in days, not weeks. Half a dozen assaults were costly on both sides, the garrison losing about 1200 men altogether and the Macedonians 56, according to Arrian, but many of those were from the command ranks of Alexander's army. Memnon and the Persians were so hard pressed that they abandoned the town of Halicarnassus itself, after putting the arsenals and buildings to the torch. There were still two citadels at Halicarnassus: an island fortress called Zephyrion and a hilltop called Salmakis, to both of which the Persians now retreated. Memnon left Halicarnassus and joined up with the Persian fleet, as mentioned before, to harass Alexander's supply lines.

Alexander razed what was left of the city to the ground, punishment for its resistance, just as he had done to Thebes. But he also instituted a new policy which was to become his standard approach in those non-Greek areas of the Persian Empire that he conquered. A native, Queen Ada in this case, was named satrap and given civil power, while a Greek garrison of 3200 was left in Caria under the command of a Macedonian officer, Ptolemy, who had distinguished himself as the commander of the territorial brigade that broke into Thebes the year before (and should not be confused with the later king of Egypt). Ptolemy's primary task was to keep up the pressure on the remaining Persian citadels, which held out until early summer of the next year, 333 B.C.E.

It was now autumn of 334 B.C.E., and Alexander decided to divide his forces. Before he could campaign much further, he had to secure both his supply lines and the interior of Asia Minor. With Memnon a threat at sea, Alexander decided to send the newly married Macedonian territorials home for the winter, some 3300 men in all, which also served to secure the land portions of his supply lines. While these men were back in Macedonia, replacements would also be recruited to join them, both to make good his losses and to augment the army. Parmenio was placed in command of the allied Greek forces and campaigned into Lydia where there were still Persian forces at large. Alexander himself, with the remainder of the Macedonians, continued along the coast into Lycia and Pamphylia. Since the bulk of the army was operating in territory in which it could live off the land, this also reduced his dependence on a long supply line and relieved his newly acquired Asian Greek allies of the necessity of supporting him in the field. Also, controlling the coast denied naval bases for the Persian fleet, though the Persians concentrated on the islands in the Aegean rather than the coasts. The army was to meet again in the spring of 333 B.C.E. at Gordion in central Anatolia.

Alexander moved along the coast, at times cutting inland in Lycia to avoid difficult coastal mountains. He made his way to Phaselis, which had marked the furthest extent of Athenian influence in the previous century. Again sending the army inland towards Side in Cilicia, Alexander himself took the coast road past Mount Climax. As he passed along the shore, a strong north wind abated the tides and eased his passage. The official historian and public relations expert for the expedition, Aristotle's nephew Callisthenes, dispatched the story that the sea had acknowledged Alexander as "Great King" by abasing itself (what the Persians called proskynesis) before him.

There are in fact several accounts of this, including the fact that Alexander fails to mention this incident in his own dispatches to Antipater. But propaganda was equally part of Alexander's campaign, and not a strange concept to the Persians. Parmenio intercepted a Persian agent at this point, supposedly treating with one of Alexander's commanders, in order to plot an assassination attempt. Alexander arrested the individual, Alexander, the prince of Lynkestis, although he was held in arrest for three years before any action was taken. Clearly, Alexander himself was unsure of the story, and a similar event would take place the next year which was without substance. This was most likely part of a Persian disinformation campaign to sow distrust and undermine Alexander's authority. Public relations worked both ways.

Having gotten as far as Cilicia, Alexander now swung north to secure sections of the king's road to Sardis and central Asia Minor. The Persians pulled into the fortress at Celaenae, and Alexander detailed 1500 men under Antigonus Monophthalmus "The One-eyed," one of Philip's old generals. Antigonus was made satrap of Greater Phrygia and given the task of reducing the Persians. More important, Antigonus was to be the watchdog who kept the communications route back to Macedonia open, a task he performed well for the rest of Alexander's reign.

It was now the spring of 333 B.C.E., and time to move on to the rendezvous at Gordion. Parmenio brought up the rest of the army, along with the 3300 men who had been on leave, as well as 3000 fresh Macedonian infantry and 500 Macedonian cavalry as reinforcements. This was the equal of two new territorial brigades and almost two full new cavalry squadrons. But with them came grim news: Memnon of Rhodes had been active with the Persian fleet over the winter. The Persians had worked their way north along the coast securing the islands off the coast of Asia Minor: Cos, Samos, and Chios.

Memnon had also been sent funds from Darius, and he in turn sent agents to stir up those Greek cities known to oppose Alexander and Macedonia, such as Athens and Sparta. This was, again, the traditional Persian policy which had worked against the Athenian Empire at the end of the Peloponnesian War, and against Sparta earlier in the fourth century. In the meantime, Memnon moved on to make an attempt on the island of Lesbos. It was a serious threat, both directly to Alexander's lines of communications (and worse so, if Memnon was to get a base in Asia Minor itself) as well as increasing the possibility of raising Greeks on the mainland against him. It was a threat that would come to reality two years later, but now and later, Alexander's response was the same: He refused to be deflected from what he considered the primary campaign against Persia.

Nevertheless, it provided the opportunity for one of most telling bits of Alexander's good fortune. In Gordion, where the army finally came together again, there was a temple to Zeus Basileus (Zeus the King) in which sat an ancient cart. According to legend, this was the cart of King Midas, who had fulfilled a prophesy by it and achieved his kingdom (and brought him the nickname Midas the Golden because of that luck). The yoke, which held the draft animals, was attached to the cart's shaft by a thole pin and held in place by a complicated knot. By tradition, whoever undid the knot would become "Lord of Asia." Alexander could not but make the attempt, and the various stories connected to the outcome mark both different aspects of his character and how people viewed him.

After considerable fumbling, according to one version from Aristobulus reported by both Plutarch and Arrian, he either struck on the idea of pulling out the thole pin (which held the yoke and the pole together) around which the knot was tied, or someone suggested it to him. This way he could get at the knot from the inside where the loose ends were. The other tradition maintains that Alexander, frustrated with his attempts, drew his sword and cut it open, since the prophesy did not say how it was to be undone. The Roman sources on Alexander, Curtius Rufus and Justin, seem to favor the latter. Arrian relates both, but strikes the central point: "when the Macedonians departed . . . they gave the impression that the prophesy about undoing the knot was fulfilled" (2.3.8). It was a brilliant ploy, probably more aimed at his own men than anything else, and justification to press on.

This Alexander did, moving northeast to Ancyra in Galatia, modern Ankara, the capital of Turkey. Here word reached him that Memnon of Rhodes had died of a fever on Lesbos. Plutarch would later write an essay, *On the Fortune of Alexander*, and this is a primary example of that good luck. With Memnon's death the Persian fleet, which was mostly Phoenician, ultimately broke up, as it lacked a commander with a vision. The immediate threat to Alexander's supply lines was lessened, though not gone. There was some discontent still in Greece, but the Persian funds, ships, and men would not be forthcoming, and the threat there abated as well. Alexander's arrangement for Asia Minor, largely under the watchful single eye of Antigonus, was equally sound. Alexander could now move directly to challenge Darius in the Levant (modern coastal Syria and Lebanon), around the bay which still bears his name in Arabic: Iskanderum (Alexandretta).

From Ancyra, through the summer of 333 B.C.E., the army moved east and then south through Nyssa and Tyana, past the Cilician gates to Tarsus on the Cidnus River along to the coast, which they reached in August. From there, Alexander could mount the next stage of the invasion. The march had been grueling, and Alexander himself was exhausted. Relaxing himself, swimming in the Cidnus, Alexander caught a cold and fever. In the meantime, Darius had moved the Persian grand army to Babylon and continued his propaganda campaign. Intelligence reached Parmenio that another assassination attempt was to be made, and that Alexander's physician, Philip the Acharnanian, was the instrument. Parmenio sent word to Alexander, who was indeed being treated by Philip with a potion to reduce the fever. Alexander handed the dispatch to Philip and drank off the potion, which was harmless, but it must have caused some nervous moments for Philip. The story again played into Alexander's image, as unconcerned by rumors and having full trust in his men.

The coastal road was a dangerous one, and Alexander spent some time securing it, moving west to Soli as a base of operations. There word reached Alexander of the collapse of the Persian forces at Halicarnassus and the recovery of the island of Cos. This meant that the potential threat from the Persian fleet continued to evaporate, though, in fact, it was far from over. In celebration of the victories and his own recovery from illness, Alexander sacrificed to Asclepius, held a parade of the army and put on a festival of athletic contests and artistic competitions: the Greek version of the USO. He then moved back to Tarsus to prepare for the next phase of operations.

The Levant

Part of Alexander's task now was to gather intelligence, and Philotas scouted out the situation. Taking a strong cavalry force, Philotas moved to the area of Hieropolis on the Pyramus River, opposite the Amanian gates, which form the main northern pass through the Mount Amanus Massif and cut off the coastal plain from the interior. Here he ascertained that Darius had moved his army from Babylon to the plains opposite the Syrian Gates, the main southern pass through Mount Amanus. This put Darius well south of the Bay of Iskanderum, essentially in front of Alexander as he moved south.

By this point, Darius was being advised by his new Greek mercenary commander, Amyntas, the son of Antiochus, who was a Macedonian exile. Amyntas' advice was to stay on the plains of Sochi before the Syrian gates, where Darius had plenty of room to maneuver and the advantage of numbers over Alexander. As with Memnon's advice previously, this advice was sound. But Alexander had spent most of the summer in Cilicia, between his illness and desire to secure the lines of communication, and Darius grew impatient. His Persian courtiers urged him to move against Alexander, north through the Amanian Gates and come in on Alexander's flank. So as Alexander moved east and south along the coast to Issus at the head of the Bay of Iskanderum, unbeknownst to him, Darius moved north and then west on the far side of Mount Amanus. The two forces passed each other on opposite sides of the mountains, and Darius slipped in behind Alexander.

Once at Issus, Parmenio urged Alexander to make it his base. From Issus, he argued, Alexander could wait for Darius to move and defend either from the north (the Amanian Pass) or the south (the Syrian Pass), whichever way Darius might attack. Caught between the slopes of Mount Amanus and the sea, Darius' larger numbers would not count for much. But Alexander was as eager as Darius for a confrontation, and Darius' last known position was to the south. As with Philip, Alexander maintained a medical service to treat the army, an unusual practice for the time. He now left the sick and wounded at a base hospital in Issus, for he intended to move quickly. Alexander proceeded toward the Syrian gates.

It was a major strategic blunder. As mentioned, Darius slipped in behind Alexander, took Issus, and butchered the sick and wounded in hospital, which was the more standard practice even within ancient armies. Darius had cut Alexander's communications and blocked any hope of retreat. But in doing so, Darius had picked the very ground Parmenio had urged before. Alexander swung around and marched north, and the first battle with Darius took place at Issus.

The estimates of the numbers in Darius' army range up to 600,000, a ridiculous figure which simply could not be supported in the field by any ancient state. This merely reflects the Greek view toward Persian forces dating back to Herodotus. It was simply more men than any Greek state or combination of states could put in the field and is best translated as simply being incomprehensible. The real numbers can only be estimated. Certainly the Corps of 10,000 Immortals, the Great King's Household Gaurds, were present, along with 15,000 Greek mercenaries commanded by Amyntas the Macedonian. The Persian Cardaces (cadets) and native levies of foot and horse probably came to another 50,000. This yields a total of about 75,000 troops (still a guess, but a more accurate one). Alexander's army amounted to no more than 35,000 men, including his light armed troops, less than half the strength of the Persians.

Darius took up position facing south, with his right flank penned in by the sea and the left by the slopes of Mount Amanus, just as Parmenio had seen. Darius and the Immortals took the center of the line of battle, with the Greek mercenaries split into two divisions of 7500 on either side, and the Cardaces likewise split into two units, one each on the right and left flanks. On the extreme left, in the ravines of Mount Amanus, the Cardaces were the anchor as the Persians didn't believe cavalry could operate there. But a small force of skirmishers was placed on the heights to threaten the Macedonians as they advanced. On the extreme right, by the sea, Darius concentrated his cavalry. He was hoping to overwhelm Alexander's left (and weakest) flank and then roll up the Macedonian lines. But all Darius did was to pen his cavalry in where it couldn't move.

Because the ground opened up a bit in front of him, Alexander was forced to commit most of his troops to a single standard phalanx line to form an adequate front. Only a small force of Greek mercenaries was held back to support that line. As before, Parmenio would command the left and center, Alexander the right. The extreme left was made up of allied cavalry and scouts. At the last minute, noticing all of the Persian horsemen opposite these men, Alexander sent the Thessalian cavalry, which normally fought with the Macedonians, to support them. This was done riding behind the Macedonian infantry line, so it was masked from Persian view. Then came the Greek allies and Macedonian territorial infantry under Parmenio. The Macedonian Guards Brigade came next, then the Macedonian Territorial and Companion Cavalry, all under Alexander on the right. Alexander sent the Agrianian javelinmen and some cavalry scouts to scour the Persians out of the heights so he could advance without worry.

The Macedonians advanced to within a bow-shot of the Persian lines. Alexander's tactics were derived from Philip: namely that the left flank advance more slowly than the right, drawing the Persian lines out to the breaking point. Alexander would then smash into the Cardaces on the right, up against the ravines, forcing a break in the Persian lines through which the Companion Cavalry would charge to roll up the Persian formation and push them into the sea.

It worked as planned. The Persian Cardaces and Greek mercenaries on the Persian right charged what they thought was a faltering Macedonian left, which exposed their flank to Alexander. The Greeks in Persian service had not been at Chaeronea, where the Macedonian right had employed this strategy. Alexander charged into the Cardaces, forcing the break in the line. As the battle line dissolved, Darius' charioteer whipped his horses off the field to save the great king, followed by the main Persian cavalry force. The Immortals and Horse Guards made a last stand to cover the retreat. [This moment in the battle forms the theme for the Alexander Mosaic, represented by an illustration in this book and the portrait of Alexander on the cover.]

The rest of the battle was bloody. One Macedonian brigade commander (taxiarch), Ptolemy, the victor from Halicarnassus, was killed, along with some 120 other Macedonians of note. Alexander's losses overall were 450. In addition, there were 4000 wounded, including Alexander himself who had been stabbed in the thigh.

The Persian losses were far heavier, especially among the Royal Guard, Greek mercenaries and Cardaces. Some 8000 mercenaries survived, meaning they had lost at least 7000. The rest is guesswork as before, but couldn't have amounted to less than 20,000: roughly a third of Darius' force. Perhaps the best mark of this is the recollection of Ptolemy, the future king of Egypt. He was an officer in the Companions and later wrote that in the pursuit they "crossed a deep gully over the bodies of the Persian dead" (Arrian 2.11.8).

Alexander Mosaic, from the Villa of the Faun at Pompeii.
This was probably a copy of an original painting by
Apelles (Alexander's court painter) later commissioned
by Cassander. It shows the pivotal moment of the Battle
of Issus as Darius fled the field. The mosaic is now in The
National Archaeological Museum at Naples.
(© David Lees/Corbis).

The Macedonians thundered into Darius'
camp, where they found a sumptuous victory
feast laid out in the royal pavilion. Alexander's
men took advantage of it, and the king remarked
that "This, I believe, is being a king!" During the
feast, Alexander and his officers kept hearing
noises from the back of the tent. Overcome with
curiosity, Alexander sent Leonnatus and some
guards back to see to things. There they found
Darius' mother, wife, son, and two daughters

(abandoned by Darius). Leonnatus assured them that Darius was safe and that they would not only be unharmed but treated as the royalty they were. The next day, Alexander and his friend Hephaistion, who was taller than Alexander, went to visit the royal family. Sisygambis, Darius' mother, made obeisance to Hephaistion, mistaking the taller man for Alexander. When informed of her error, she begged forgiveness for not recognizing the king. Alexander laughed off her mistake, and raised Sisygambis up. He would later marry one of Darius' daughters.

Alexander spent the day after the battle visiting the wounded, and clearly the bloody nature of the affair prevented any immediate full-scale pursuit. But Parmenio was sent out after Darius with a special detail and tracked him as far as Damascus in Syria, some 200 miles away. The great king eluded him, but Parmenio captured the Persian baggage train and campaign chest containing some 2600 talents of silver in coins, another 500 pounds in silver bullion, and gold plate weighing 4600 pounds. To put this in perspective, remember that the normal annual income of the Athenian empire at its height had been around 1000 silver talents. Along with the 3000 talents taken in the Persian camp at Issus, this meant that Alexander would not be short of funds from this point on. The name of Issus was changed to Nikopolis (Victory City), to commemorate the battle.

Alexander appointed satraps for Cilicia and what the Greeks called Coele (or Hollow) Syria, by which they meant Lebanon. Alexander then continued down the coast rather than resuming the pursuit of Darius. A number of things had been happening at sea which forced this course.

Amyntas the Macedonian, who had led the 8000 Greek mercenary survivors from Issus, had first fled to the hills and then to Tripoli in Phoenicia. There he seized some of the Persian ships which had been laid up for lack of crews, burned the rest, and fled to Egypt. A large force led by a recalcitrant Macedonian was not to be ignored. Likewise, what was left of the Persian fleet was operating under two Persian commanders, Pharnabazus and Autophradates. They had managed to reinforce Chios and Cos, and even retake Halicarnassus once the Macedonians had withdrawn for the Issus campaign. Leaving a small covering squadron, the much-reduced Persian fleet of some 100 triremes sailed to the island of Siphnus in the central Aegean to meet with King Agis of Sparta. Agis was plotting an uprising against Antipater and the Macedonian settlement in Greece and wanted money and ships. It was at this point that the Persian commanders got the news of Issus. Agis was given thirty talents and ten ships, which he sent on to the main mercenary recruiting market at Taenarum. Pharnabazus and Autophradates returned to Asia Minor, fearing renewed support for Alexander there.

The majority of the Persian fleet by this time was made up of Phoenician (Lebanese) crews. By continuing down the Phoenician coast, Alexander at the very least expected to prompt those ships and men to come home to defend their cities. In fact, a significant number of Phoenician towns, as well as towns from the island of Cyprus, came over to Alexander. As they did so, the Persian fleet dissolved.

Alexander had reached Marathus, about a third of the way down the coast, by late 333 B.C.E. Here Alexander supposedly received a letter from Darius defending his actions against the Macedonian king and asking him as a fellow monarch to let Darius ransom back his family. According to Arrian, Alexander offered to restore them to Darius without conditions, but Darius would have to come and ask for them. Regardless, from this point on Darius would have to address Alexander as the King of Asia. The exchange of letters is doubtful, and Darius' letter may have been entirely made up by Alexander's propaganda staff. Nevertheless, it made Alexander's intentions clear. He wanted it all. Yet, Alexander ignored Darius for the next two years, which gave the Persian king time to regroup his forces again into superior numbers and pick his battlefield, another major strategic blunder by Alexander that his army and luck would make right later.

In January of 332 B.C.E., Alexander continued south, and town after town came over, including Byblos and Sidon, without a fight. This brought Alexander to Tyre, which also submitted itself to Alexander's orders, by which they meant an alliance. Tyre consisted of two cities: the newer city sat on an island half a mile offshore, and had been built when Tyre became a naval and trading power; the older Bronze Age city stood on the mainland opposite. A famous temple to Herakles Melkart stood on the island, and to convince himself of Tyre's complete submission, Alexander announced that he wished to worship in the island's shrine. Still playing both sides, hoping to maintain some neutrality perhaps, the Tyrians were determined that neither the Persians nor the Macedonians would occupy the island fortress. It was a polite request for unconditional surrender. The Tyrian reply that Alexander was free to worship at the Heraklian shrine on the mainland was a polite refusal. What followed was illogical.

Alexander claimed that without Tyre, they could not deny the Persian fleet the bases it needed, and so the city constituted a threat to the Macedonian supply and communications. This was a threat Alexander had all but ignored in Asia Minor and on the road to Issus. Further, with the submission of the Phoenician towns, the Persian fleet for all intents and purposes no longer existed. A blocking force could have been left, as elsewhere behind him in Asia Minor, but Alexander felt insulted. He would waste the next seven months there, in a costly effort that was basically unnecessary.

The siege of Tyre was a formidable undertaking and one of the most famous. King Nebuchadnezzar of Chaldaean Babylonia had besieged the town two and a half centuries earlier and even after thirteen years had failed to take the island. The half-mile distance between the island and the mainland lay across shallows no more than twenty feet deep. Today, the island is part of a peninsula connected to the mainland by a causeway. This was the result of a mole, 200 feet across, built from the mainland out to the island by Diocles, Alexander's chief engineer. Further, in order to attack the seaward side of the island city, Alexander reconstituted his fleet. Some 220 naval ships and merchantmen (lashed together to support siege towers) were mustered, with no evidence of the Persian fleet that supposedly justified this venture anywhere in sight.

As time went on, the fighting grew both bitter and nasty. Tyrian swimmers tried to pry apart

the coffers into which stones were placed to con
struct the mole. In doing so, they captured
Macedonian soldiers and crucified them on the
walls before Alexander's army. Crucifixion was
the Tyrian state form of execution, which they
passed on to their colony on the north African
coast: Carthage. The Romans picked it up from
there. It is an excruciating form of torture, in
which it normally takes up to six days to die and
in which the victims ultimately drown as their
lungs fill up with liquid during prolonged expo-
sure. Alexander began executing Tyrians in retal-
iation. The Tyrians responded with fireships to
set the works ablaze. The siege dragged on.

When the final assault came from both land
and sea, Alexander personally led the Guards
Brigade into the breach in the wall from the mole
itself. The Tyrians fell back to make a stand at
the shrine of Agenor, but by now the Macedonians
were over the seaward wall as well. The Tyrians
sought refuge in the Temple of Herakles Melkart,
but the rest was simply mopping up. Some 8000
Tyrian soldiers were killed, including 2000 crucified on the walls by the Macedonians in turn as
an act of revenge. The rest of the males captured
were massacred, though the Sidonians, appalled
at the savagery in taking the city, smuggled
15,000 out of Tyre. Thirty thousand women and
children were sold into slavery. The Macedonians

lost some 400 men in the entire siege, and twenty-one of the Guards Brigade in the final assault.

It was now August of 332 B.C.E. and the situation in western Asia had decidedly shifted in Alexander's favor. What was left of the active Persian fleet was destroyed at Tenedos (the rest deserted). Alexander's forces in Asia Minor had retaken Lesbos, Chios, and Miletus. Most conspicuously, Antigonus the One-eyed had defeated all attempts to cut the supply lines in Asia Minor. What Alexander didn't know was that opposition was gathering in Greece itself, the seeds sown by King Agis of Sparta.

But western Asia was firmly in Alexander's hands, and Darius acknowledged it. A firm offer reached Alexander at Tyre: 10,000 talents for the return of Darius' family and the cession of all land west of the Euphrates River, and his daughter's hand in marriage, which would legitimize Alexander's rule in Persian eyes. It was more than even Philip had planned, and Parmenio urged Alexander to accept it. Alexander replied that were he Parmenio, he would accept. As he was Alexander, he would instead reply as follows: He needed no funds from Darius, and they were his anyway; nor would he accept a mere portion of Darius' lands, instead of all of it; and if he (Alexander) wished to marry Darius' daughter, he would do so with or without Darius' permission. Essentially, it was the same public reply Alexander had made before Tyre, with the same audience in mind and the same propaganda purpose. There being no diplomatic opening left to him, Darius now began to prepare in earnest for a final confrontation.

Alexander determined to round out the western territory of Asia by taking Egypt. He moved quickly past Mount Carmel and along the coast of Israel and Judah to the Gaza strip. This marked the western end of the Sinai road to Pelusium: the gateway to Egypt.

Egypt

The key to this area was the city of Gaza itself, the Persian commander of which was a eunuch named Batis. The city's other main importance was as the major shipping point for Arabian incense, used for religious purposes throughout the East and the Mediterranean. Batis enlisted a force of Arab mercenaries and prepared for a long siege. Gaza city stood on a mound about two and a half miles from the sea, surrounded by desert to the landward side, and shoals along the coast. A long siege was what Batis got: two months.

There were four main assaults on the walls of Gaza, on the third of which Alexander himself was severely wounded in the shoulder by a catapult bolt that penetrated both his shield and breastplate. The attacks took place along a huge mound constructed against the Gaza wall. The siege engines from Tyre arrived shortly after Alexander was wounded.

Alexander now ordered his engineers to build a mound as a fighting platform 440 yards across and 250 feet high all around the circuit wall of Gaza. Sappers mined under the walls in several places and collapsed the tunnels, which therefore breached the defenses in several places. The Macedonians poured in and tore down the gates. The mercenaries and men of Gaza expected no quarter. It was a miniature repeat of Tyre. The men were all slain and the women and children sold into slavery: symbols of resistance to Alexander. But the road to Egypt was now open, and Alexander took it.

Alexander crossed to Pelusium in just six days and was met there by his fleet. It was now November of 332 B.C.E. The Persian satrap of Egypt, Mazaces, did not have sufficient forces to resist Alexander. Most of the initial Persian garrison had joined Darius' army prior to the Battle of Issus. Amyntas and the Greek mercenary survivors from Issus had fled to Egypt, but Amyntas had been killed in a dispute with some natives and the mercenaries had moved on to Crete. Equally, Mazaces was disturbed not only by the loss at Issus, but Darius' behavior there. So he welcomed Alexander and opened Egypt's cities to him.

Alexander's march became a triumphal progress, and he was welcomed by the Egyptians as a liberator. He put a garrison in Pelusium and sent the main force on directly to Memphis, where the Nile valley and delta meet. Alexander himself marched to Heliopolis (ancient On) and then on to Memphis. Along the way he took care to keep the Egyptians' good faith by sacrificing to their gods, especially to Apis the Bull, the chief fertility god. This was a marked difference from the Persian policy, which had twice deliberately killed the Apis bull to punish Egypt.

Once at Memphis, he continued the sacrifices and again held a series of athletic contests and artistic competitions, importing performers and professional athletes from Greece for the occasion. The road to Egypt had been long and hard, and this amounted to Greek rest and recreation, as the games at Soli in Cilicia the year before had been. It was probably here and now that Alexander was formally recognized as Pharaoh of Egypt.

Alexander spent the winter of 332-331 B.C.E. in Egypt. He moved down the Nile from Memphis and across the delta to the westernmost mouth of the river. Here at the Egyptian city of Rhakotis, across Lake Mareotis, Alexander decided to found a new city. Insulated from the harsh Egyptian climate, this stretch of land had a Mediterranean climate which was much more temperate than either the Nile delta or valley. Further, it was ideally located to be the link between Egypt and the Aegean. The city was named, according to Macedonian custom, after the king: Alexandria, the name it still bears.

Alexander's instincts were confirmed almost immediately. Word reached him now that the last of the Greek insurgents in the Aegean islands had been put down and the Persian naval forces destroyed. Tenedos, Chios, Cos, and all of Lesbos were firmly under Macedonian control. The Persian naval commander, Pharnabazus, had been captured but had escaped. Nevertheless, there now was no Persian fleet. Alexander spent the winter of 332–331 B.C.E. in Egypt.

Philip's original plans had been to unite the Greek world (*oikumene*), and part of that world was five Greek colonies, independent poleis, on the coast of Cyrene (the modern Libyan bulge). In early 331 B.C.E., Alexander moved out along the coast to round off his control of the Greeks, but the five cities sent word of their submission. This embassy reached Alexander at Paraetonium, modern Mersa Matruh, along the same coast road fought over by Britain and Germany in World War II.

Alexander then decided to turn south and visit the Oracle of Zeus Ammon at the Oasis of Siwah, which was famed throughout the East and

Greece. Arrian maintains that this had been Alexander's prime goal all along, as he had been seized by a "pothos" or undeniable urge to do so just as he had been to see the Danube. The Oracle at Siwah, according to tradition, had been consulted by the mythological heroes Perses, before his fight with the Gorgon, and Herakles, the founder of the Argead royal house. It certainly would be in keeping with Alexander's heroic image of himself, and his devotion to his family's mythic past. The two versions, one practical (Cyrene) and the other romantic (Siwah) are not in fact mutually exclusive.

During the course of the trip, the army got lost. In Ptolemy's account two serpents found the army and led it to the Oasis. Aristobulus makes it two ravens (sacred to Zeus) that guide the army. As Alexander approached the temple, the chief priest greeted him as the son of Zeus Ammon. Later historians, both in antiquity and in modern times, have made much of this. Supposedly this is the beginning of Alexander's obsession with deity and ultimately his own deification. If so, it was a bit late, for as Pharaoh he had been addressed as this by all Egyptians since the previous autumn in Memphis.

Alexander prayed for the aid of the gods (according to Plutarch) consulted the oracle in private (according to all the sources), and one can therefore only guess about what: an omen for his new city, Alexandria?; his destiny as Lord of Asia?; the upcoming campaign against Darius? He wrote to his mother, Olympias, that he had discovered something very interesting and that he would tell her about it when he got back. However, he never returned to Macedonia or saw his mother again. The whole incident is one of those things from which both people who admired and who hated Alexander, ancient and modern, have spun off what they would like to reinforce their points about his character. It raises more questions than it will ever answer and must remain part of Alexander's mystique.

Alexander returned from Siwah to Memphis, where there were a number of Greek embassies awaiting him. In addition, Antipater had sent some reinforcements: 400 mercenaries and 500 Thracian mounted scouts. This places the time as still in the winter of 331 B.C.E., as in the early spring Antipater was faced with a rebellion in Thrace by a Macedonian commander, which Antipater crushed. This Thracian episode was a mis-timed part of a larger conspiracy on which Agis of Sparta had been working for more than a year. Using Persian gold and hiring mercenaries, including Greek survivors of Issus, Agis was joined by most of southern Greece, but markedly not by Athens. He mustered an army of some

20,000 infantry, plus the 8000 mercenaries, and 2000 cavalry. By the summer of 331 B.C.E., it was a serious threat to Alexander's settlement of Greece, the League of Corinth, and his own supply line. But Alexander was not to hear of this until after he had left Egypt.

For the rest, Alexander set up the government in Egypt. Local autonomy was to be allowed to the Egyptian provinces (nomes) under native leaders so long as they paid their taxes. The military command in Egypt was split among several officers, to prevent any one of them from being too powerful, as were the finances. Egypt was a tremendous resource for both supplies, since Greece was threatened and Egypt was closer, and money. Alexander then began to make preparations for the march east and the decisive battle for Asia.

I V

Alexander and the Eurasian Empire

Introduction

"As spring began to reveal itself" in 331 B.C.E., Alexander at last began the march east to confront Darius. He had with him an army of 40,000 infantry and 7000 cavalry. At the same time, the fleet made directly for Tyre. From Memphis, Alexander marched along the coast road for Phoenicia, after bridging the Nile and canals to ease the passage of so large an army. His fleet and army met up again as planned at Tyre, where Alexander held another formal review and put on athletic games to rest and entertain his men. As he had done in Egypt, Alexander made arrangements for the governance of the Levant. Satraps and garrison commanders were named for the region, and a new central secretariat to handle all financial matters was established under one of the Companions, Harpalus.

Alexander's long absence from Greece was beginning to cause problems. Faced with a Greek allied army of 30,000 in the Peloponnesus, Antipater asked Alexander for aid. Given the coming battle with Darius, there was little Alexander could do in regard to troop reinforcements, but the fleet and monies were available. Under the command of Amphoterus, the fleet was dispatched to Crete (probably to cut off the supply of mercenaries to Agis), and a second squadron of 100 triremes was raised in Phoenicia and Cyprus to aid the few Peloponnesian cities that remained loyal to the Macedonian cause. Funds were sent directly to Antipater. That at least stopped the growth of the Greek allied forces, and probably answers the question of why Athens chose not to join them. Nevertheless, as Alexander turned inland, he was unsure of the outcome of this "Lacedaemonian War" as Arrian called it. Indeed, he would not find out about the outcome until well after the Battle of Gaugamela.

Alexander set out from Tyre, at first retracing his steps north, then moving east through the Syrian Gates to Thapsacus on the Euphrates, which he reached by late July or early August. While all of this was going on, Antipater had scraped together an army of 40,000 troops, mostly old men and boys, to pit against Agis. Antipater moved south to challenge the Greeks in the Peloponnesus itself, rather than see the rebellion spread. The opposing armies met at the city of Megalopolis, just north and west of Sparta, in one of the bloodiest battles in Greek history. The rebellious Greeks left some 5300 dead on the field, including Agis, but at the cost of 3500 dead from Antipater's forces. A thousand of those were Macedonians, more than Alexander was to lose in all of his main battles for Asia put together. Nevertheless, Alexander's good luck had held, and Antipater had won the day. Alexander would not be bothered by a Greek rebellion again in his lifetime.

The Gaugamela Campaign

Alexander found the Euphrates River bridges defended by Mazaeus, the Persian satrap of Babylon, with a force of cavalry and Greek mercenaries. But Alexander had approached so quickly that Mazaeus fell back. The obvious route for Alexander now was to move south, down the Euphrates, to Babylon. This was the nearest royal residence and the center of Persian administration for all of Mesopotamia (modern Syria and Iraq): a place Darius would have to defend. Instead, Alexander marched north, up the Euphrates toward the Armenian highlands, specifically because

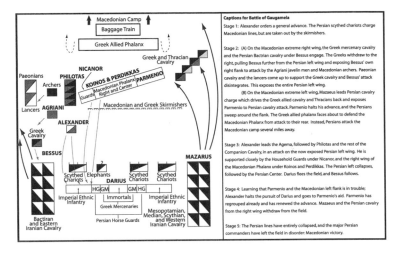

Battle of Guagamela

it provided fodder for the horses, and supplies were easier to come by there. It also broke the desert heat, which was lessening as autumn drew on. The Macedonians then turned eastward across the Syrian Desert, with the intent to cross the Tigris River and march down the far side toward Babylon.

On September 17, Alexander began crossing the Tigris and then halted for four days in the ruins of Ninevah to rest the army. He also needed intelligence: information on the position of the Persian army and other forces. At the end of the four days, Alexander's scouts reported enemy cavalry on the plains to the south (the date is fixed for the night of September 20 or 21 by a lunar eclipse). The next day, taking with him the Agema, another squadron of the Companions and his Paeonian scouts, Alexander himself led the way, with the rest of the army close behind. Moving quickly over the next four days, this reconnaissance force drove the Persian scouts back and captured some of them alive. From these men, Alexander learned that Darius was a few days' march further south, with a large force.

Indeed, Darius had been about fifty miles away, just north of Arbela near the village of Gaugamela. Here he had chosen a relatively flat plain on which his large army could maneuver. The estimates for the size of this force are even more ludicrous than those for the Battle of Issus: one million foot soldiers, 40,000 cavalry, 200 scythed chariots, and a small force of Indian war elephants. Given that it was the full Persian levy, the size of the mounted forces is not unreasonable, but the numbers for the infantry are. We can presume that the 10,000 Immortals were there, as well as whoever was left in the Greek mercenary corps. Estimates here range from 6000 to 20,000, the latter being far too high. The true numbers must have been about 10,000 to 12,000. There were also some 30,000 Persian cardaces as well. At most then there were 50,000 foot soldiers, no more than 20,000 of which could be classified heavy infantry. Added to the mounted forces, the whole army could have come to about 100,000, more than twice the size of Alexander's forces.

Once Alexander had captured the scouts, he held up again for four days, both to wait for the rest of the army to come up and to make sure they were all fully rested for the coming battle. He pitched a camp, with a ditch and palisade to house most of the baggage and those men not fit to fight because of illness or the rigors of the march. On the twenty-ninth, he set out at night with the rest of the army drawn up for battle expecting to fight Darius at dawn. But the two armies were still about seven and a half miles apart. Alexander moved carefully for a change, and when they crested a line of hills about four miles into the march, he found Darius on the plain drawn up in battle array. A quick officers' conference was held, and Parmenio urged Alexander to pitch camp and scout out the terrain for the upcoming battle, which he did.

Darius had had his sappers preparing the plain, sweeping it of obstacles to allow his chariot corps and cavalry to operate easily. In doing so, he also had created the ideal conditions for Alexander and his phalanx. The Great King had also made no attempt to hide his dispositions as he had expected Alexander to go immediately into the attack. The foot soldiers were drawn up as they had been at Issos, with the Immortals and Darius in the center, flanked by the Greek mercenary corps on each side and then by the Cardaces, also on each side. Though his forces were formidable in overall numbers, Darius in fact had fewer heavy infantry than Alexander, but they were drawn up across a broad front to stretch Alexander's lines as thin as possible.

It was in cavalry that the Persians greatly outnumbered Alexander, more than five to one. These were drawn up in deep columns on the flanks, with Mazaeus, the satrap of Babylon, commanding the right wing, and Bessus, the satrap of Bactria, over the Scythian and Bactrian cavalry on the left wing. In front of the army were the 200 scythed chariots, which Darius counted on to break the Macedonian line. Not knowing Alexander's intentions, and fearing a night attack, which indeed Parmenio urged on Alexander, Darius kept his men at arms all through the night. They were exhausted when the next day came.

Alexander exhorted his men in a short speech, stating that unlike their previous battles, this next one was for all of Asia and that he had no doubts of their courage and devotion. Orders were issued for the next day, and all were told to turn in, as Alexander himself intended to get a good night's sleep. In the morning of September 30, Alexander drew up his forces, with himself and the Companion Cavalry on the right wing along with a small force of Greek mercenary cavalry and the scouts opposite Bessus. Next to him was the Guards Brigade under Parmenio's son, Nicanor, and then three of the Macedonian territorial brigades. The remainder of the Macedonians stretched out to the left wing, commanded by Parmenio, with the Greek allied cavalry on the extreme left flank. The Greek allied infantry was mustered as a separate full phalanx line behind the Macedonians, where they could either reinforce Alexander and Parmenio, or face about and defend them from the rear, should Darius threaten to break around them.

Alexander ordered the army forward, with his own right wing in advance just as he had done at Issos, the design being the same: to draw the Persian lines taut and then break them. As a result he encountered Bessus and the Scythians first. Squadron after squadron of Persians in deep formations hit Alexander's lines, but Arrian says that "the Macedonians stood up to the charges, and (counter)attacked vigorously . . . and broke their lines." Darius now ordered the chariots to attack, but these proved an utter failure. Alexander's light-armed troops speared the drivers and pulled the reins of the horses, flipping the chariots. Those few chariots that got through had no effect, as the Greeks simply opened their lines as they moved forward, allowing the chariots to pass to the rear, where the Macedonian grooms from the camp brought them down.

Now both lines were fully engaged, but as Darius' line advanced in the center and right, he unwittingly handed the battle to Alexander. Darius' left line, as at Issus, was punctured, and Alexander wheeled the Macedonian cavalry and the Guards Brigade to the left and set out straight for Darius himself. The fighting was at close quarters, with the Macedonians "shoving the Persians and hitting at their faces with spears." Darius, who now "saw nothing but horrors all about, was first himself to turn and begin to flee," followed quickly by Bessus and the rest of the left wing.

Just as Alexander was setting out in pursuit of Darius, however, word reached him that Mazaeus' cavalry had been successful in flanking the Macedonian left wing. The Greek allies had faced about to defend the Macedonians' backs and ultimately restored order in the camp to the rear, where the Persians had stopped to loot. Nevertheless, Parmenio sent for aid. Alexander turned back and fell on the Persians from behind, while Parmenio, who had already restored the line in front of the Persians, was now advancing as well.

This trapped the Persians between them. Arrian says that this was the hardest fighting of the whole day, and by this point Mazaeus' division was the last of the Persians off the field. The battle was over and the Persians in complete rout.

The Persian losses were terrible; the lowest estimate (which is from Curtius) set them at 30,000 dead. The estimates of the Macedonian losses (taking into account all the sources) range from 100 to 500 at most. It was the greatest victory in Greek history. Alexander rested the cavalry until midnight and then set out after Darius.

The Pursuit of Darius

Darius fled south to Arbela and then eastward through Armenia to the northern Zagros mountains into Media. He presumed (correctly) that Alexander would reason that the Persian royal party would continue south and east to Susa and then to the Persian capital at Persepolis. With Darius went Bessus and the Bactrian cavalry, along with what was left of his bodyguard, the Immortals and some 2000 remaining Greek mercenaries. But Darius was forced to abandon his chariot, shield, and treasure.

The pursuit was brutal. Taking only his cavalry, and leaving the rest to follow on, Alexander covered some seventy-five miles by the end of the next day but failed to catch Darius. He continued on toward Babylon, Arrian stating that the Persians killed in the pursuit were around 3000, but far more were taken prisoner along with the rest of the chariots and the Indian war elephants. In this march alone, Alexander lost 100 troops, half of whom were from the Companions, and more than 1000 horses, which made it as costly as any pitched battle.

As he approached Babylon, Alexander expected a fight, but instead was met by Mazaeus and the Babylonian priests before the city. Mazaeus had given a good account of himself at Gaugamela and was disgusted with Darius' behavior. As a result he surrendered the city, fortress and treasury of 50,000 talents to Alexander. This marked the beginning of a new policy. Alexander reappointed Mazaeus as satrap, but with a Macedonian named to command the garrison and a separate Greek financial officer responsible to Harpalus. The same was done for the satrap of Armenia, who voluntarily surrendered his province. Persians who cooperated were to be kept in civil authority, but Macedonians and Greeks would always look after the military and the money. Finally, Alexander ordered to be restored all the Babylonian temples previously destroyed by the Persians, especially that of Marduk Bel, the chief god, to establish a policy of religious tolerance.

By this point the cavalry was rested, and the infantry had caught up with them. Alexander set out along the royal road east to Susa, at the main southern pass through the Zagros, still assuming that he was pursuing Darius. On the way, he received envoys from the satrap of Susa surrendering the province and city. As was now his custom, Alexander reappointed the Persian satrap, but only in civil authority and with Macedonian garrisons and army commanders. It took three hard weeks of marching to reach Susa, so Alexander paused here to rest his men. Unaware of Antipater's victory at Megalopolis, he also sent 3000 talents to Antipater to aid in putting down Agis, before he resumed his pursuit.

By now it was January of 330 B.C.E., and Alexander still moved south. After forcing his way by a night march past a difficult hill position, Alexander split his forces. He sent Parmenio along the royal road to Persepolis with the Greek allies and the baggage train, while Alexander took the Macedonians to the Persian Gates by the mountain route. There Ariobarzanes, the satrap of the province of Persia, had gathered an army of 40,000 infantry and 700 cavalry. This was the first resistance Alexander had faced in months. He left Craterus with two brigades, some cavalry, and the archers to attack (on Alexander's signal) the wall that Ariobarzarnes had built across the pass. Meanwhile, Alexander made another night march around the mountains to attack the pass from the flank. He overcame several sets of guards and then signaled Craterus. Attacked on all sides, the Persians abandoned the position and fled to the hills. The way into Persia itself was now open.

Alexander marched south, first to the capital of Cyrus the Great at Pasagardae and then on to the royal palace of Darius the Great at Persepolis, where he joined up with Parmenio. In the course of this march from Susa, Alexander had taken three royal residences, each with its own treasury, and with them some 180,000 talents of silver, not counting gold, jewels, and silver plate. In coins alone, that was enough to run the Athenian empire at its height for 200 years. He was now fabulously wealthy, but he also knew he had missed Darius. Alexander prepared to go into winter quarters at Persepolis.

It had been a hard year's campaigning, and Alexander indulged the Macedonians with feasting to relax. In the course of arranging their entertainment, to entice Ptolemy's Athenian mistress, Thais, to dance for them, Alexander offered to grant her whatever she wished. That turned out to be the burning of Darius the Great's royal palace to avenge the burning of Athens 150 years before. Parmenio argued against it on the grounds it was now Alexander's palace and it might convey the idea to the Persians that he was just a conqueror intending to pass through, rather than their new ruler. Not for the first time, Alexander ignored Parmenio's sound advice. The palace was destroyed, never to be rebuilt. Its ruins exist to this day.

More important, this incident demonstrates several things. First, Alexander was still not yet thinking as Great King, that is, as the successor to Darius. That would soon change. Second, unparalleled success had made Alexander even more willful; the destruction was irrational. But who could say no to him? Finally, there was a rift beginning between Alexander and Parmenio in particular, but also with some of his Macedonian officers as well. Clearly, Alexander had no plan in mind as yet for how he would rule or incorporate this new Persian territory; they were now far beyond any project that Philip II had imagined. It was a problem that would grow in the future.

In the spring of 330 B.C.E., as the snows cleared from the passes into Media, Alexander renewed the pursuit of Darius. He marched toward the royal summer palace at Ecbatana (modern-day Hamadan). Darius had managed to gather some 7000 talents, 6000 infantry, and 3000 cavalry, but clearly was in no shape to offer any resistance. As he retreated into Iran proper, Darius became the virtual prisoner of Bessus of Bactria. The best he could hope was that he would be the figurehead of Persian resistance; in fact, his days were numbered.

When Alexander reached Ecbatana, he paused long enough to take stock of the new world that was emerging. He had destroyed the Persian imperial power and taken all the major royal residences. He now declared that the war between the Greeks and Persians was over, the offensive purpose of the League of Corinth fulfilled. From now on, he intended to campaign in his own name and for his own purposes. The Greek allied forces were dismissed, with their pay, booty, and a gift of 2000 talents from Alexander to share among themselves. Any who wished to join up as mercenaries were welcome to do so, and Arrian comments that many did. The rest were escorted back to the sea and home.

He appointed a Persian as satrap in Media, but left a garrison of 6000 Macedonians under Parmenio, who was also charged with pacifying the surrounding region. Harpalus and the royal treasury were established there as well. Alexander began minting coins in his own name bearing the symbol of the Persian griffin. He was finally acting as the legitimate government of Persia, but he still had to get Darius.

Alexander organized a fast-moving column of the best cavalry and most fit infantry and set out after Darius. He wanted to be king of Asia in name as well as in fact. In eleven days this force covered a huge distance, fifty miles on the last day alone as it carried them past the Caspian gates onto the Iranian plateau. On that last day, the advance guard caught up with Bessus and Darius' party. Rather than have Darius fall into Alexander's hands, Bessus ordered him killed and fled on to Bactria (part of modern-day Afghanistan). Conveniently, the story was spread that Darius was still alive when the Macedonian officer in command found him. He was given water, but the Great King died before Alexander came up. As he died, supposedly, Darius gave his signet ring to the officer to pass on to Alexander. The story may be too convenient, but whether given or taken from a dead man's hand, the ring gave Alexander the legitimacy he wanted and finding Darius dead saved Alexander considerable trouble. Instead of a martyr to Alexander, Darius was one to his own rebels. His body was sent to Persepolis and buried with full royal honors, as Arrian states, "as the other kings who had ruled before him." In both Persian and Macedonian custom, the burial of one's predecessor established one's own legitimacy. Alexander could continue the war now as the Great King and avenge his predecessor.

The Guerilla War in Afghanistan

With Darius' death, all central authority in the Iranian plateau and Afghanistan disintegrated. Most of the native satraps tried to reestablish their holdings as the independent chiefdoms they had once been before Cyrus the Great. Bessus, however, claimed to be the Great King and successor to Darius III, taking the royal name Artaxerxes IV. This gave real purpose to the new campaign, the repression of another rival. But the nature of the warfare changed. Rather than fight pitched battles against the Macedonians, which Alexander had demonstrated were useless, each of the satraps fought his own war of hit-and-run tactics from remote strongholds or mountain fortresses.

Alexander was eventually forced to split up his army, with independent columns operating under Coenus, Craterus, Ptolemy, and others. Wherever the native satraps surrendered to him, Alexander reappointed them as before, with Greek military garrisons and commanders. But several satraps held out against him: primarily Bessus Great King; Satibarzanes of Aria; Oxyartes of Sogdiana; and Spitamenes, one of the Sogdian tribal chieftains. For now Alexander pursued Bessus, but the war was spread out. Individual columns and garrisons were attacked.

Collection of artifacts from Tomb II at Vergina, including a gorytus (combined bow case and quiver for arrows) from Scythia, pectoral, greaves, and a series of disks decorated with sunbursts from the *pteriges* (leather strips) which hung down below the corselet to protect the area from waist to midthigh. The sunburst was a common symbol, but especially to the Argead Royal House, as it reflects their foundation legend. (Photograph by Winthrop Lindsay Adams, taken at the Archaeological Museum at Thessaloniki.)

It took Alexander almost a year to get Bessus and suppress Satibarzanes in Aria. He ultimately drove Bessus across the Oxus River (the modern-day Amu Darya), into what are now the independent republics of Central Asia. But Bessus slipped back into Afghanistan and fled to Spitamenes. Too hot to handle, Spitamenes offered to surrender him in an effort to convince Alexander of his loyalty, but in fact Spitamenes continued his rebellion. In the end Spitamenes may merely have told Alexander where Bessus was to remove a rival.

Ptolemy captured Bessus and, according to Alexander's instructions, placed him bound, naked, and confined by a wooden collar on the roadside where Alexander and the army would pass. Alexander questioned Bessus publicly about his treason in killing Darius, had him whipped while his crimes were announced, and his ears and nose cut off for claiming the kingship, all according to Persian custom. Bessus was then sent off for another public trial in Ecbatana for killing Darius, and there he was executed, again according to Persian custom.

But the guerilla war continued until 327 B.C.E. The problem with fighting a guerilla war was that the insurgents relied on the local populace for supplies, recruits, and above all, information about the opposing forces. Scattered over vast distances, hitting in many bands ranging in number from mere raiders to forces that could threaten whole cities, the trick was to deny the guerillas those supplies, recruits, and information. The most successful tactic against guerilla warfare was to watch the supporting populace so none of those vital elements could be supplied to the enemy. That meant either herding the population into places where one could observe and control them or establishing garrisons in existing centers to do the same thing. The Romans called them *castella*, or little fortresses, in Africa and Britain, when dealing with similar tactics. In turn, the British called them concentration camps in the Boer War in South Africa at the turn of the last century and in Malaysia in the 1950s. The Americans called them strategic hamlets in Vietnam, and had used similar tactics in the Philippine Insurrection and the Huk Rebellion of the 1950s. Alexander called them cities.

He now began a policy of city (polis) foundation, which more typically meant refounding existing towns and placing in them as colonists and citizens mostly Greek mercenaries. In effect, this gave him a permanent garrison, but also began a process of incorporation, as these Greeks married into the local families and established a new elite. They also could watch over the subordinate populace. Alexander had picked up a new supply of Greek mercenaries by accepting into his forces those surviving mercenaries from Persian service, another new policy. These were added to the mercenaries already serving with him, most of whom had come from the former Greek allies.

At least two dozen such cites were founded, most, though not all, named Alexandria. Many of these towns still exist, and indeed are fabled in the history of central Asia. They include

Alexandria Areion (modern Herat); Alexandria Arachosia (modern Kandahar); Alexandria Maracanda (modern Samarkand); Nikaia, which means "Place of Victory" (modern Kabul); and Alexandria Eschate, which means "at the End of the World" (modern Khojent) on the Scythian frontier of central Asia. It established altogether a Greek frontier and political presence which was to last in the region for 300 years.

But such a policy takes time to put into effect. In the meantime the war continued, sometimes under extraordinary circumstances. The rest of 329 B.C.E. and early 328 B.C.E. were taken up campaigning in Bactria and along the Scythian frontier, operating out of Alexandria Maracanda (Samarkand) as the main base. The Scythians and Bactrians had been the core of Bessus' command at Issus and now did the same for Spitamenes, until the Massagetae killed him in an effort to appease Alexander. A force of "Macedonians who scattered to forage were cut down" by a massive raiding force of 30,000 (Arrian 3.8). Alexander pursued them to a mountain refuge that he took by frontal assault. Only 8000 of the rebels survived; the rest were killed in the fighting or committed suicide by throwing themselves off the rocks.

Alexander had placed Macedonian garrisons in the seven cities along the Jaxartes (Syr Darya) to form a frontier against Scythia and planned to build a central city to control the region: Alexandria Eschate (Khojent). Fearing this, the inhabitants "seized and killed the Macedonian soldiers garrisoning the cities," having been put up to this by Spitamenes. Alexander reacted immediately and in two days had overwhelmed five of the cities. Those inhabitants not killed outright were enslaved. The sixth city, Cyropolis, he took by a surprise attack through the sewers, killing some 8000 defenders and forcing the remaining 15,000 to surrender. The last city fell on the first attack, and none of the defenders were left alive.

While Alexander was occupied on the frontier, Spitamenes took the opportunity to attack the base camp at Maracanda. Alexander sent three separate relief columns there, while he stayed to lay the foundations of Alexandria Eschate, raising the walls to the city in some twenty days. But one of the forces, some sixty Companion Cavalry and 800 mercenaries under Caranus, was ambushed by Spitamenes and wiped out. In response to this, though he was suffering from dysentery, Alexander marched immediately to Maracanda, covering 180 miles in three days to relieve the city. The hit-and-run nature of the campaigns against the Macedonians on the Scythian frontier, and in Bactrian and Sogdiana, as well as Alexander's reactions, are all hallmarks of guerilla warfare, and typify the campaigns of the next two years. It was hard, unpopular fighting, with little booty or glory to be had.

This brutality on both sides was symptomatic of more than the warfare of the times, but rather is the norm for guerilla warfare and national struggles in any era. It has led one modern historian to refer to it as "ethnic cleansing" by Alexander, which is evocative of the viciousness of the struggle and relating it to modern times. At the same point, it overlooks the fact that Alexander did not kill on a strictly ethnic basis, as he at the same time incorporated those tribesmen who accepted his rule. And far from forcing them to give up their religion and customs, he tolerated them, honored them, imitated them, and incorporated them into his armies. In all things, Alexander remained complex and hard to explain.

By 328 B.C.E., the struggle had moved on to the rebellion of Oxyartes in Sogdiana, which was conducted in much the same vein as before. But by now the policy of city foundation was paying off. More areas were incorporated and co-opted into Macedonian rule. The rebellion had been largely suppressed in Aria, Bactria, and along the Scythian frontier. The most spectacular event against Oxyartes was Alexander's assault on the Rock of Sogdiana, with which this biography opened. A select mountain assault force of

300 scaled the heights, with Alexander promising a reward of twelve talents to the first man up, as well as rewards for those who followed. They achieved total surprise, at the cost of thirty dead in the climb, and the Sogdians simply surrendered.

The guerilla war was winding down, but in the end it was not brought about by simple military victory, but rather through a traditional Macedonian policy first used by Alexander's father, Philip II: marriage and incorporation. Oxyartes' wife and daughters were captured at the Rock and were treated with honor by Alexander. He fell in love with one of the daughters, Roxane, and sought to marry her. Hearing this and the manner in which his family was accepted, Oxyartes came to Alexander and was "honorably treated" by Alexander, and so the wedding was celebrated. As news of this spread, the last stronghold surrendered to Alexander by the spring of 327 B.C.E., completing the pacification of Afghanistan.

Alexander began to reorganize the army to incorporate the tribesmen of Afghanistan. He had, of necessity, already begun replacing his horses with the larger local breed. In the course of his campaigns, he had continued to receive reinforcements for the territorial brigades from Macedonia, while promoting some of those into the Guards Brigade. In all, some 45,000 Macedonians had joined since the original expedition. Still, Alexander could not expect to continue to drain Macedonia at this rate. To make allowance for this, he had already ordered some 30,000 of the Persian Cardaces to be equipped in the Macedonian fashion and to begin training in phalanx tactics. The Companion Cavalry was now divided into four Hipparchies of 1000 men each, to be commanded by Hephaistion, Craterus, Perdikkas, and Demetrius. The lead squadron of each unit was Macedonian as before, but squadrons of Bactrians and Sogdians filled out the rest.

The phalanx was now brought up to its full ten territorial brigades, and for the moment remained solely Macedonian. Only three of the original taxiarchs, however, were left. The campaigns had been hard, and to an extent the guerilla war had changed the Macedonians' attitudes. Up to the fighting in eastern Iran, there had been no particular prejudice or rancor against the natives or Persians in the campaigns. The course and nature of the fighting in Afghanistan brought the prejudice out in both officers and enlisted men. It amounted to a growing Macedonian reaction, first to being in eastern Iran, and then to Alexander himself. And Alexander had changed.

The Macedonian Opposition

To some extent there was always some opposition to Alexander. Plutarch remarks that the summer after Philip's death, 336 B.C.E., Macedonia was plagued with unrest. A brief bloodbath had been part of the follow-up to the assassination, which included some very convenient, and not necessarily justified deaths. Persian propaganda and plots had emerged from the beginning of the expedition, hyping rumors of possible assassination attempts. There were Macedonians like Darius' mercenary commander, Amyntas, among the Persians forces. And there had been a tendency on Alexander's part to belittle Parmenio, probably because the old general was a living symbol of Philip II and the army he built.

As Alexander continued to move east, he paid little heed to the structure of empire. For the most part, he merely adapted the satrapal system. Initially, Macedonians were appointed as governors. Then natives such as Ada of Caria were established, with reliable Macedonians in charge of the garrisons. In Egypt, multiple commanders were named. From the beginning of the Gaugamela campaign, a central financial office was established (a true innovation), but the political and military structure remained the same. From Babylon on, Persians who submitted kept thcir officcs, but always with Macedonians in charge of the military.

All of this was haphazard, jury-rigged to facilitate the continuing of the campaigns eastward, always eastward, further from the sea and home. None of it appeared planned in any way, which bothered those who remembered Philip. Moreover, Alexander's actions became increasingly puzzling, such as the destruction of the palace at Persepolis and the dismissal of the allied Greeks. Parmenio, well into his 70s, had been left behind in Ecbatana. His son Nicanor, the commander of the Guards Brigade, died in the course of the long pursuit of Darius. So comfortingly familiar figures were disappearing, for Parmenio had always been a voice of reason and a reminder of Philip to the Macedonians. And then the guerilla war began, hard and uncertain fighting far from home. His staff were becoming disturbed about how they were to hold such a vast empire with so few men, especially now that the native opposition seemed to be stiffening in Afghanistan.

The first signs of this dissent emerged in 330 B.C.E., soon after the death of Darius. While supressing the rebel satraps, first in Aria and then in Drangiana, Alexander came to Phrada. While there, some minor members of the court hatched a plot against Alexander. According to Justin, this was because of Alexander's growing tyranny. But whether for grandiose or personal reasons, word of this was taken to Philotas, the commander of the Companion Cavalry. Philotas dismissed it, largely because of the circumstances in which the information was gathered and the people involved. Alexander found out about it independently; he arrested, questioned, and executed Philotas for treason, along with the accused plotters.

The whole incident is open to a wide variety of interpretations, but there are a number of things to note. First, Alexander was prepared to believe that Philotas, by not acting immediately, was guilty. Alexander's father had been killed in just such a minor plot to which no one paid heed. Second, there was discontent among even some of the minor officers. And third, in the aftermath, Alexander struck out against those who didn't agree with him. Agents were dispatched to kill Parmenio, Philotas' father, back in Ecbatana. Parmenio had dedicated his life to Macedonia and the Argead monarchy, two of his sons had died in Alexander's service, and he had trained most of the army's officers. His death was not popular, and most of the ancient sources on Alexander condemn him for Parmenio's death.

What then were the reactions among his contemporaries? On learning of this, Antipater, Alexander's regent for Europe, asked: "If Parmenio was guilty, who is to be trusted? If he was innocent, what is to be done?" In the immediate aftermath, Alexander sent word that some of the veterans were to be sent home and asked them to write letters home stating this, which Alexander would send with his own dispatches. Alexander then confiscated and read them, looking specifically for those which expressed disaffection with him. The men who wrote such letters he put in a special unit used for extremely dangerous assignments as punishment. The opposition was real, and Alexander himself knew it.

To counter some of this discontent, much of which grew from the guerilla war and being so far from home, Alexander struggled to make things seem more familiar. He brought the royal pages out from Macedonia and established favorite pastimes, such as hunting, and court ritual. Religious festivals were held as if they were back in Macedonia. All these measures did was to provide a counterpoint. To anyone who has served overseas, it is clear that the more someone tries to make it like home, the less like home it seems. Independence Day, Thanksgiving, or any national or religious holiday from any culture, in a far-away land becomes more poignant and out of place.

In the winter of 328 B.C.E., Alexander was in Samarkand and the court celebrated the festival of the Divine Twins, Castor, and Pollux. A banquet was held, at which Arrian states that "the drinking went on for a long time." During the proceedings, a Greek *poetaster*, a kind of stand-up entertainer, made fun of some of the Macedonian commanders who had been defeated by natives in the ongoing guerilla war, to the amusement of Alexander. Kleitos the Black, the commander of the Royal Squadron, got angry and told Alexander that such talk wasn't right. In the following exchange, Alexander called Kleitos a coward, and Kleitos answered that it was "this cowardice of mine that saved your life" at the Granicus and "that it was by the blood of Macedonians . . . that you have become so great" (Plut. 50.6). Kleitos was expressing the opinion of the Macedonian senior commanders, and when he began comparing Alexander unfavorably with Philip, the argument degenerated into a brawl. Friends dragged them apart and pulled Kleitos from the hall. But Alexander grabbed a spear from one of the guards, dashed after him, and ran Kleitos through.

Alexander was disconsolate and according to some sources, even attempted suicide. He sulked in his quarters for several days. His friends pleaded with him to come out, and the army became alarmed, for who wanted to be left in the middle of Afghanistan with no Alexander? Whether he was genuinely sorry or just trying to draw attention away from the murder of a popular officer, the public show of grief worked and the crisis passed. But it again marked growing discontent.

At the same time, Alexander had a genuine political and cultural dilemma on his hands. He was now both Great King of Persia and King of Macedonia. This meant that at times he had to adopt the Persian dress and ritual expected by his native subjects. But his Macedonians, even the most common troops, called him simply "Alexander." The Macedonian tradition was that the king was "first among equals." All Macedonian citizens had the right of direct and frank petition (free speech) before the king. The subjects of the Great King begged to be heard and fell flat on their faces before the royal presence, a practice called *"proskynesis."* It was difficult to treat all equally, when one group of Persian nobles was groveling before him and the rawest Macedonian recruit called him by his first name. Further, while such an act was common eastern ritual, and did not imply any divine nature to the ruler, for the Greeks it was a religious ritual and one rarely performed even before the gods.

In the spring of 327 B.C.E., Alexander made an attempt to blend the court rituals together and carefully discussed it with his inner circle. At a private gathering where no ritual was required, some Persians nevertheless voluntarily performed the *proskynesis*. Macedonian reaction

was to break out laughing because it seemed ludicrous in that situation. Callisthenes of Olynthus,
the expedition's spin-doctor and Aristotle's
nephew, gave Alexander a speech to that effect,
with which most of the Macedonians agreed.
Sources say as much. Under the circumstances, it
was humiliating to Alexander, but it again points
to the presence of an opposition to the direction
that Alexander had been taking. From this point
on, Alexander tried to maintain a dual policy.
For all matters dealing with Persian rule and custom, Alexander worked through Hephaistion,
who was now appointed as *"Chiliarch"* (for all
intents and purposes, the Persian imperial prime
minister). He was simply the Great King as they
had always seen him. For Macedonian relations,
he used Craterus as his chief minister. As with
the rest of the governmental structure, it was
only a stopgap measure. The problem remained.

Even in Afghanistan, however, Alexander was
not removed from traditional Macedonian court
intrigue. At a court hunting party, one of the royal
pages anticipated the king's first cast of a spear, a
breach of etiquette. The page, Hermolaus, was
whipped as a matter of discipline in accordance
with Macedonian custom. He took this as a personal insult and hatched a plot among some of
his fellow pages to kill Alexander. The whole incident was inflamed by a lecture of Callisthenes,

who was also tutoring the royal pages, on tyran-
nicides, the killers of tyrants: an unfortunate
choice of topic.

Ptolemy found out about the plot, and with the
example of Philotas before him, decided to tell
Alexander immediately. The pages involved were
arrested, tried, and stoned to death according to
Macedonian custom. Callisthenes was imprisoned and eventually died. Though this incident
in many ways resembles both the Philotas affair
and the assassination of Philip, the point is that
on many levels there was opposition to Alexander.
This was ongoing and was prompted by everything from the usual grievances, which had always been present, to specific quarrels with the
situation in the guerilla war and the changing
nature of Alexander in the face of success.

But that guerilla war was coming to an end in
327 B.C.E. with the marriage of Alexander to
Roxane. Some of the tension might have been relieved. Alexander would have time to turn to or-
ganizing the empire, dealing with the problems
of merging the two kingdoms. After all, essentially royal governance for both Macedonians
and Persians was based on personal relationships. Instead, Alexander was drawn further
eastward (as he himself said) by an undeniable
urge (*pothos*) to see the eastern limit of the
Ocean. Not a reason as easily understood by his

Macedonians as was the war with Persia. They were just going further away.

The Indian Campaign

Though the resistance in Sogdiana (what is now central Afghanistan) itself had ended, to approach India Alexander had to move east into much more mountainous terrain. This is the area of what is today northeastern Afghanistan and northwestern Pakistan, the tribal territories that have been a refuge for Al Qaida. Here Alexander split the army into two columns. One, under Hephaistion and Perdikkas, consisted of most of the Macedonian territorial brigades and mercenaries and was to secure the route down the Kabul (Cophen) River and through the Khyber Pass into India. India is a term that in antiquity simply referred to the Indus River valley and the Punjab, the five tributaries of the Indus, what is modern-day Pakistan.

Alexander took his favorite troops, primarily the Guards Brigade and Companion Cavalry, and forged a route north of the Kabul through the mountains. The orders were to use all the military muscle necessary to overwhelm the opposition and set up city foundations and garrisons to control the region. In essence, it was precisely what they had been doing in Bactria and Sogdiana, but now done to stop any guerilla activity before it started.

The columns set out at the end of spring of 327 B.C.E., the forces spreading out to sweep the territory in front of them and then concentrating on dealing with any resistance. At one of the first of these, across a river "called Choes," Alexander was wounded slightly in the shoulder by an arrow. But when the Macedonians assaulted the town, whether by Alexander's orders or out of their own frustration, they not only killed those who resisted, but massacred the captives and destroyed the town itself, a habit formed in the guerilla war. The next town surrendered immediately.

In this fashion, Alexander bulled his way through the mountains. He fought no open pitched battles, but rather a string of assaults on mountain citadels. The most famous of these was against the legendary Aornos, which supposedly even Herakles, the mythic founder of Alexander's dynasty, had failed to take. As with the Rock of Sogdiana, all resistance and obstacles were overcome, and Alexander came to the upper Indus River. Here he constructed boats, and the army sailed downriver to join Hephaistion's column by February of 326 B.C.E.

While Alexander worked his way by his own track through the Hindu Kush and to the Indus River, Hephaistion and Perdikkas took the more normal route and reached the Indus River well ahead of Alexander. The engineers built a bridge across the river and waited for Alexander. Hephaistion had also built a squadron of small boats and two thirty-oared vessels, presumably to protect the bridge. By the time Alexander arrived, the native ruler of the western Punjab, Taxiles, had sent 200 talents, 30 war elephants, 3000 oxen, and 10,000 sheep to reprovision Alexander's army. He formally submitted his capital, Taxila, to Alexander and kept his kingdom within a satrapy now controlled by a Macedonian governor. Equally, Taxiles provided an allied contingent of cavalry, 800 strong, as scouts and guides for the expedition, And so Alexander crossed through India.

Up to this point, Alexander had been unopposed. But in the central Punjab that changed. Poros, the local ruler of the territory across the Hydaspes River (the modern Jhelum), not only refused to submit, but intended to stop Alexander from crossing the river. Poros had an army of 300 heavy chariots, 200 war elephants, 4000 cavalry, and 30,000 light infantry. The most troublesome element of this force was the elephants. Horses have to be trained to work with elephants, otherwise the elephants' scent makes the horses unruly. Further, the elephants themselves are difficult to attack. They have thick hides, and hitting them with arrows merely enrages them. Rather than charge, they stampede and can be used to break up infantry formations. The Indian practice was to put a gondola (platform) filed with archers on top of an elephant as well. Up to this point, the Macedonians had seen very little of these beasts. There had been a few at Gaugamela, and Taxiles had already sent thirty of them to Alexander. But their use would be a nasty surprise for the Macedonians.

Alexander had no intention of forcing a direct crossing. Instead, as he had done at the Danube, he scouted upriver about eighteen miles and found a ford. Taking the Companion Cavalry and horse archers, as well as the Guards Brigade along with two territorial brigades and light armed troops, Alexander made a night march. He had with him about 5300 cavalry and 10,000 infantry of all types. The rest he left under Craterus to make a show of preparing to cross the Hydaspes, hoping to hold Poros in position and thereby surprise him with a flank attack. It almost worked.

Alexander did cross, but Poros got word of it. Some 2000 Indian cavalrymen, under Poros' son, fought a delaying action in which the son was killed. In the meantime, Poros left some elephants and infantry to prevent Craterus from crossing and marched to confront Alexander on the Karri Plain. He drew the army up with the elephants in front and the infantry behind them in the center, with the cavalry in two units of 2000 each on the flanks.

The elephant screen was a new problem for Alexander. He likewise put his infantry in the center under the Guards commander, Seleucus, and light armed troops on the flanks. But he placed all of the cavalry on his right wing. The horse archers had orders to tie up the Indian infantry beyond the cover of the elephants, while the cavalry destroyed the chariots and their counterparts on the Indian left. Until then, Seleucus was not to advance.

The battle was fierce and filled with unexpected moves. Poros tried to bring his right wing cavalry across in front of the elephants to save his left wing. Alexander anticipated that, and 2000 Companions crossed behind the phalanx and fell on the Indians from the rear. The Indian cavalry retreated through the elephant line. This proved the toughest fighting of all, and the Macedonian infantry now advanced to encircle Poros as his cavalry, chariots, and elephants were all knocked out of the battle. Poros fought on gallantly until personally isolated. Alexander invited him to surrender and asked him how he would like to be treated. "Like a king," Poros answered. He was.

It was a costly battle. Poros had lost all of his chariots, all of the elephants (killed or captured),

3000 cavalry (including his son), and 20,000 infantry. Alexander lost 280 cavalry and 700 infantry, mostly among the elephants. In addition, Alexander lost his favorite horse, Bucephalus, whom he had ridden for twenty years. Alexander founded a city in his honor: Bucephala. Alexander also celebrated his victory by founding a city called Nicaea (place of victory) on the site and commissioned a special set of commemorative medallions, some of which still survive. Poros was eventually appointed the satrap of the region.

But it was still not the end. By now it was May of 326 B.C.E., and Alexander first rested the army for a month, then moved on across the modern Chenab and then on to the Hydroates River (the modern-day Ravi) into the area of Kashmir. Resistance was stiff, and the army spread out to overwhelm the region, and then concentrated on taking the central city of Sangala, somewhere near modern Lahore. This was done by assault, but at a cost to Alexander of 100 dead and 1200 wounded. It wasn't getting easier.

Alexander continued east to the final river in the Punjab: the Hyphasis (the modern-day Beas). At last an end, of sorts. But what awaited them was not the ocean as expected, but the Ganges Plain and the subcontinent of modern India. Alexander's scouts told him that the land was good, but also it was populous, filled with a warlike people and many, many more elephants. Arrian states that "This report encouraged Alexander with a desire to go on further." He also says that the Macedonians' spirits failed them, "seeing the king taking on task after task and danger after danger." The Macedonian opposition to further adventure and doubts about what they were doing had now reached the men themselves.

The men held informal meetings throughout the camp. Some merely complained in general, while others stated that they "would go no further." Alexander got wind of this and called an officers' conference to which Alexander made a carefully worded speech, but failed to evoke the hoped-for response. Instead, he got a sullen silence, with everyone pointedly staring at the ground. Eventually, Coenus spoke up for the whole army, stating that for the very reason that great things had been achieved, which had been Alexander's theme, it was necessary "to set some limit to the labors and dangers" which the men had faced now for eight years. Few of the original band were left, many died of sickness, and all the rest "were wearied in body and spirit." They longed to see their parents, wives, and children, and their homeland again. The speech was greeted with applause, many of the officers actually weeping at the thought of going home.

Alexander's reaction was anger. He dismissed them, then called them again the next day and said he was going on regardless, but would compel no one to accompany him. Let them leave him alone among his enemies. Once again he got silence. Still he took the omens for crossing the Hyphasis and continuing; for once they were all bad. Alexander gave in to the logic of the situation, and announced to the army that he had decided to turn back. His announcement was greeted by shouts of joy and weeping.

Alexander divided the army into twelve parts, each of which erected an altar the size of a tower to one of the Twelve Olympians (the major gods of the Greek pantheon) to mark the limit of their passage and to make thanksgiving for their victories. Sacrifices were held in commemoration. Alexander held games and cavalry exercises for the men to celebrate and relax. Then he turned down the river and began the march back. The great expedition was over.

V

The Last Days and World Legacy of Alexander

Introduction

While Alexander had been forced to give up his desire (*pothos*) to see "Ocean," he was never to forget it. Indeed, he now turned back to the Hydaspes (Jhelum) River with the intent of taking the army down the Indus precisely because he thought that this was the source of the Nile. He had seen crocodiles and vegetation along the Indus that had reminded him of Egypt and confirmed the speculation in his own mind. In due time, Alexander discovered that the Indus emptied via two mouths into the Great Ocean, the Indian Ocean, and therefore was not the source of the Nile. But all that lay ahead.

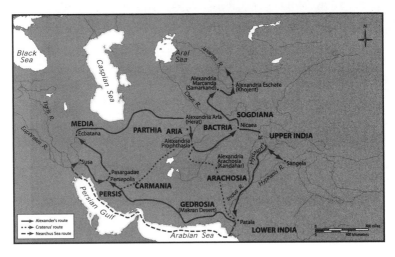

Eastern Asia

Nevertheless, for the purpose of sailing down the Indus, Alexander had a fleet built of some eighty thirty-oared war galleys (*triakonters*) and more than 800 supply, transport, and horse-transport vessels. Before they set out, Coenus, his second in command, died of a fever and was buried with full honors. Alexander also had to make arrangements to settle the government of the region before he left. He appointed a satrap for the land west of the Hydaspes (Jhelum), which protected the route into Afghanistan and Persia. But Alexander turned the Indus valley itself over to Poros as king and ally, hoping that local autonomy would be the key to stability.

In November of 326 B.C.E., Alexander then divided the army, and embarked with his family (Roxane had accompanied him), the Guards Brigade, the Agema of the Companion Cavalry, the archers, and the Agrianian javelinmen (his favorite mercenaries) onto the vessels. Craterus took a force consisting of one Macedonian territorial brigade of infantry and most of the cavalry down the right bank of the river. Hephaistion took the bulk of the army, including 200 war elephants, down the left bank to screen them from hostile tribesmen. And so they set out for home.

The Road Back

If the army thought that the way back would be easier, they were sadly mistaken. Alexander seemed to go out of his way to find confrontation, almost as if he were taking out his anger at having to end the expedition on the army itself. Or possibly he was trying to reassert his control over men who had, before this, been willing to follow him anywhere.

Wherever there was a hint of resistance, Alexander spread the army out from the ships in several columns to crush it. The tactics were the same as had been used successfully in the guerilla war in Afghanistan, and in fairness to Alexander he may have thought it as necessary in this instance as it had been before. It would not be the last time that such tactics linked the areas of Afghanistan and Pakistan together. But the carnage involved was tremendous, and even Arrian commented on its severity.

The first area Alexander passed through was Malli, and it was the toughest. Every fortress, every town was a target. One such city, with a largely Brahmin, or high-caste, population, virtually died to the last person, and Alexander had to rally his men personally to kill them. After that, the Macedonians found the towns of Malli deserted. Alexander pursued those populations even across desolate terrain. The army moved down the Jhelum until it joined the lower Ravi (Hydroates) River and on into the area of the Oxydracae.

The fighting in this area was equally fierce, the more so because the surviving Malli had joined the local tribesmen. At one citadel, when Alexander's men lagged behind in the assault, he again personally led the ascent up the scaling ladders. Alexander was closely followed by his shield bearer, Peucestas, who held the shield of Achilles taken from Troy at the beginning of the expedition, Leonnatus, one of the bodyguards, and a sergeant (*dimoiritos*) named Abreas. But the ladders broke under the rush of the Guards Brigade behind them, leaving Alexander's small party alone.

Isolated on the wall and exposed to arrows from all about, Alexander jumped down on the far side. The three others who made it to the top joined him. An arrow in the face killed Abreas, and Alexander was severely wounded by an arrow in the lung. Peucestas stood over him with the shield of Achilles, along with Leonnatus, against all comers. Some Macedonians, seeing Alexander cut off, broke up the ladders and used them as climbing pegs in the wall to ascend and relieve the group defending Alexander. Others tore at the gates or broke through postern doors, so that in small and then larger packets they passed into the city. They slaughtered everyone in the town: man, woman, and child. It was a mark of how frightened the army was at the prospect of losing Alexander, but hardly an excuse.

The tribes that had resisted now began to surrender, and others sent envoys to submit before any confrontation. Alexander recovered from his wound and continued by ship down to the main branch of the Indus. On the lower Indus, Alexander encountered light and scattered resistance, most of which ceased at the first assault. Large areas simply submitted, and so by July of 325 B.C.E., Alexander reached Patala in the Indus delta. He spent some time refortifying the site and rebuilding the harbor along Macedonian lines. He also set about pacifying the region. He appointed a Macedonian, Peitho, as satrap of the lower Indus. As with the area west of the Hydaspes, this was to keep the vital communications with Persia open.

At this point, Alexander redivided the army. Craterus was to march back on the main road through Arachosia to Carmania and Persia. With Craterus went several Macedonian territorial brigades and most of the older veterans whom Alexander planned to discharge and send back home. More ships were constructed, worthy of an ocean voyage, and placed under the command of Nearchus, the Cretan. He would take the severely wounded and sick back through the Indian Ocean and up the Persian Gulf. Alexander would take the rest by the coastal road and through the Gedrosian (Makran) Desert, though why is anyone's guess. There was no strategic reason for it, and he could simply have taken the route along which he sent Craterus. The route through Gedrosia would be a long, hard march. Alexander apologists have argued that it was to establish supply depots for the fleet, or alternately, by the fleet for the army. In any event, the fleet left a month earlier than expected because of native unrest. It was the wrong season for sailing, and the fleet arrived considerably after the main columns were back in Persia. Nearchus stated in his memoirs that this march

was another *pothos* (undeniable desire) by
Alexander, like the one to see Ocean or the
Danube. Or possibly it was precisely because it
was a difficult way that only truly legendary figures could cross and so it appealed to Alexander's
sense of the heroic. Regardless, all three columns
were to join up at Susa in Persia, which was accessible to the fleet by river and to the marching
columns by the royal roads.

The journey was both fascinating and horri-
ble. They encountered strange primitive peoples,
something that had always intrigued the Greeks.
But mostly they found only scant supplies of
food and water, and what water they found was
brackish. Though the satraps and commanders
in the area had been ordered to send supplies,
none were forthcoming. The army was plagued
with sandstorms. Arrian states that thirst killed a
large number of the baggage animals, and even
more were killed by the Macedonians themselves
as supplies of food ran out. This only made matters worse, as there weren't enough animals then
to carry the army's materials. These then had to
be abandoned. When the monsoon season hit,
their problem was too much water. Flash floods
carried away many of the women and children
among the camp followers. As they moved inland, the heat and lack of water returned. Out of
86,000 who began the long march in Alexander's

column only 25,000 came through. It was the single worst disaster of his reign.

At one point in the march, only a helmet-full of water could be found, with nothing else in sight. It was brought to Alexander, but instead of drinking it, he poured it out as a libation to the gods. A brilliant bit of psychology, Arrian reported that this was as good as a drink of water for everyone in the army. Water was found and the army marched on into Carmania, where they ultimately joined up with Craterus. After resting, the forces again broke up into separate columns and continued by several land routes back to Persia. India and the long march were now behind them, but Alexander still had one major category of problems to confront. He could no longer avoid dealing with how he would control such an empire.

The Problems of Empire

There were, in fact, several immediate crises in government facing Alexander on his return, mostly caused by his prolonged absence, some of which were demonstrated in the lack of supply dumps on the march back from India. Over the course of the rest of 325 B.C.E. and early 324 B.C.E., as Alexander approached Susa, he dealt with these harshly. First, those satraps and commanders who had failed to send supplies as ordered for the long march across the Makran

were punished. Then it became clear that the
Persian satraps in Media and in the province of
Persia itself were conspiring, most having presumed that Alexander was not coming back
from India. Their obvious goal had been to take
power themselves. These provinces comprised
the heartland of Persia. In all, some six of them
were relieved of their posts and executed as examples. There had also been several outright
rebels with whom he had to deal. Four more
satraps were arrested over the next few months
and were awaiting punishment when Alexander
himself died the next year, 323 B.C.E. in Babylon.
By the time Alexander reached Susa in February
of 324 B.C.E., a significant portion of the men
he had left to govern as satraps and generals,
both Greeks and Persians, had been eliminated.

Worse, Alexander's chief financial officer,
Harpalos, proved no better. Having set himself
up as a virtual king in Babylon, freely using the
monies in the central accounts for his own purposes, Harpalos now decided to flee before
Alexander could have him arrested. He hired
some 6000 mercenaries as a guard, took 5000
talents of embezzled funds, and commandeered
thirty triremes. Harpalos fled to the Peloponnesus and called on Athens to give him asylum.
But he was too hot for even Athens to handle;
they took his offer of 700 talents, but arrested

him. Harpalos eventually escaped and fled back to Crete in 324 B.C.E., where he was assassinated by one of his own mercenary officers. The whole incident merely proves how widespread the problem was.

Alexander appointed new satraps and commanders, but his problem, and the core of the Macedonian opposition to Alexander, was how to govern in the long term. At Susa, he decided to marry the daughter of Darius III, Stateira, and Parysatis, the daughter of Artaxerxes III Ochus, probably to legitimize his position among the Persians. He used the occasion to celebrate weddings between his Macedonians and Persian families on a grand scale. The ceremony itself was conducted according to Persian ritual. Some eighty of his officers took brides from among the highest Persian noble families, and his friend Hephaistion married another daughter of Darius. In all, 10,000 of his Macedonian troopers married Iranian women as well, many recognizing relationships of long standing. Alexander put on a wedding feast that lasted five days and paid the dowries of the brides himself. His present to his men was to pay off their private debts, to the tune of some 20,000 talents.

The long march back had significantly reduced the numbers in the army, and specifically in the Royal Corps. Persian cavalry were added to the Companions to fill out their ranks, not as before in distinct squadrons, but fully into the existing Macedonian units. Before the Indian Expedition, Alexander had ordered the 30,000 Persian Cardaces (cadets) trained in the Macedonian fashion and equipped with the same kinds of arms as the Macedonian phalanx. These troops now reported to Susa. A new model army was emerging that fully represented both peoples: a new union, supplementing the weddings.

In a sense, Alexander was actually following Macedonian principles and practice. Philip had done the same things with his frontier policy and this was just an extension of that. The political definition of being a Macedonian citizen had revolved around holding land from the king in exchange for military service. This fulfilled that. None of this sat well with his Macedonians, displaying a prejudice probably confirmed in the guerilla war in Afghanistan and the ghastly campaign in India.

Hephaistion had been appointed chiliarch during the guerilla campaign in Afghanistan. The term chiliarch is Greek for the "commander of a 1000-man unit (a regiment)," but here it is used in the Persian sense derived from the commander of the Great King's personal guards and who functioned as the "prime minister." Alexander continued his policy of city foundations, settling, in particular Greek mercenaries into new populations. This was not entirely popular with the mercenaries, and some revolted. It proved a continuous problem, though not a major threat. It was just another problem for which Alexander had to find a solution. This he did in a special decree read out at the Olympic Games by a personal envoy sent by Alexander, the adopted son of Aristotle, Nicanor of Stagira. Word of the "Exiles Decree" had gotten out and some 20,000 Greeks who had been exiled from their home cities showed up for the event. Alexander ordered the cities of the League of Corinth to take back their own political refugees in *homonoia,* and Antipater as general for Europe was to see to it. It secured a place for those mercenaries who wished to return to Greece.

Except among the exiles themselves, this was not a popular order for either the cities that had to take these men back, in many cases bitter political rivals whose property had been confiscated and would now have to be returned, or for Antipater who had to enforce it. That very likely is the reason for the second decree announced at Olympia, which if anything was even more controversial than the first. Alexander claimed divine honors, specifically that he was to be worshipped "as if he were a god." This tends to disturb modern sensibilities more than it would those in ancient Greece. Figures from Greece's mythic past had been humans accorded divine honors: Herakles the hero, Dionysus the god of fertility and wine, and Asclepius the god of physicians, for example. Alexander's accomplishments rivaled these, indeed at times literally took place in the mythic footsteps of Herakles and Dionysus. For that matter, Alexander's father had been moving in this direction when he was assassinated at a "festival of the Olympians." In general, this was the celebration of a truly extraordinary life and amounted to the ancient version of canonization: His soul would go through an "apotheosis" and reside with the gods on Olympus. But it was something that would have taken place after death.

Modern scholarship on Alexander's Deification ranges from the opinion that it was proof positive that Alexander had become a megalomaniac to apologists seeking a practical reason for Alexander doing this. After all, divinity was an essential concept for the Pharaoh of Egypt, and who but a "god" could enforce something like the Exiles' Decree. It is one of those questions about Alexander which will always be debated, and which tells us more about the people making whatever case they have about it than it does about Alexander himself. What is interesting is that the contemporary reaction was no different than the modern one. Antipater thought it was impious; the Athenians immediately complied and set up a cult; and the Spartans simply stated that "If Alexander wants to be a god, let him be a god." It was no concern of theirs.

Back in the East, in the meantime, Alexander had moved from Susa to Mesopotamia which he intended as his headquarters. Hephaistion led the army down to Opis on the Tigris River, about 200 miles above Babylon, and Alexander joined him after a yachting trip downriver from Susa. At Opis, Alexander continued reorganizing the army, which included plans to send some 10,000 of the older veterans home. This touched off a heated exchange. The veterans felt they were being dismissed to make room for the new Persian corps trained in the Macedonian fashion. All the resentment about seeing enemies accepted as equals, the rigors of the guerilla war in Afghanistan, the horrors of India, and the march back boiled over. Alexander had been acting more and more like the Persian Great King, which he was, and more distant. They marched to the king to express their grievances, as was the Macedonian custom and as they had done on other occasions including at the Hyphasis in India. Most sources, especially the Roman ones, refer to this as the "Mutiny at Opis," though it is doubtful the Macedonians saw it that way. They just wanted to go home, all of them, and for Alexander to take them there.

This time, however, Alexander flew into a rage. He jumped down into the crowd from the dais on which he was meeting with his officers and pointed out the leading spokesmen for immediate arrest as ringleaders. Alexander had resentments of his own and expressed them. In the speech rendered in Arrian, Alexander told them that his father, Philip, "found you wanderers and helpless, clothed in sheepskins, pasturing your sparse flocks on the hillsides." Philip gave them cloaks to wear ". . . and brought you down from the hills to the plains"; he gave them victories and "made you dwellers of cities, gave you good laws and customs." In doing so, Alexander was drawing a parallel with what he was trying to do in governing Persia.

Alexander then moved on to himself, cataloguing the victories he had given them in Asia Minor, Coele Syria, Egypt, Mesopotamia, Afghanistan, and India. During all of that he shared their hardships, ate the same food they ate, slept as they slept ". . . save that I wake before you that you may sleep in your beds quietly." Then Alexander called out to them ". . . here, let any of you carrying wounds strip himself and display them. I also will show mine, for I have no part of my body, in front anyway, that is left without scars." Alexander reminded them that he had led them through every hardship ". . . through every land, every sea, every river, every mountain and plain." He had even married as they had married, "and the children of many of you will be blood relations to my children."

Now he had the intention of sending home those who were beyond the ability to campaign, "to be the envy of all." But since they all wanted to go, then, "*Leave, all of you!*" And when they got back to Macedonia, they were to tell them "that this your King Alexander, victor over the Persians, the Medes, Bactrians, Scythians; conqueror of the Uxians, Arachosians, Dragianians; lord of Parthia, Chorasmia, and Hyrcania to the Caspian Sea; who crossed the Caucasus Mountains beyond the Caspian Gates, the Rivers Oxus and Jaxartes, and the Indus as well, that none but Dionysus had crossed, and then the Hydaspes, Acesines, Hydroates and would have crossed the Hyphasis *had you not shrunk back* tell them that you took yourselves away, and left him to the barbarian tribesmen you had conquered." Such a recitation would "no doubt make you seem glorious among men and pious in the sight of the Gods! *Go away!*"

Alexander left the dais and returned to his quarters, leaving orders to not be disturbed. The army stood there in stunned silence. Arguably, this is one of the great speeches in classical literature, though it is debatable how much of it may really be Alexander's. But the army's reaction does not stem from the rhetoric. They were shocked at Alexander's reaction; they had never seen him lose his temper, nor reject them. In its way, the "Mutiny at Opis" is far more revealing of the changes in Alexander than the "Deification Decree." He was acting more like a Persian than a Macedonian king.

For three days Alexander kept them at a distance, though they stood before his tent begging forgiveness and, more importantly, to be heard. Alexander finally relented, and the new spokesmen began to go over their grievances, the very items that Alexander's temper tantrum had short circuited three days before. The first of these was that Alexander treated some Persians as if they were kinsmen, which of course many were, by marriage, and Alexander stopped them and said, "But I make you all my kinsmen." They raised a shout and a victory song, and dropped the rest of the list. By a grand gesture, Alexander had diffused a sticky situation. The ringleaders under arrest were quietly killed, and nothing more was said about them.

Still, Alexander had the problem of integrating both his *personae* as Basileus of Macedonia and Shah-in-Shah of Persia, as well as blending the

Greeks and Persians together. To celebrate the happy end of the incident and reconciliation, Alexander held a great feast for both the Iranian and Macedonian elements, some 9000 guests in all. But the Macedonians were seated in the inner circle around Alexander himself, as a gesture of respect. Alexander had another point to make. As host, Alexander mixed the wine and water in the great *krater* and offered the prayer as all of them, Macedonians and Iranians alike, poured out a libation. According to Arrian, Alexander "prayed for all sorts of blessings" but especially for "*homonoia* [harmony and equality] and *koinonia* [common cause or fellowship] in his reign among his Macedonians and Persians."

Modern scholarship about this reconciliation has ranged from the idea that this was an expression of Alexander's altruistic hope to unite East and West to it being a cynical attempt to gloss over what Alexander considered a temporary problem. The former points to the language of the event, the latter to the fact that no policies indeed changed and that it was just rhetoric. The truth lies somewhere in between, and the key to it is in Alexander's Macedonian background. The Persians and Macedonians were united in being under Alexander's rule (*arche* as it was expressed in the prayer), and such rule in both traditions was based on kinship and custom.

Alexander was related by blood and marriage to both Persians and Macedonians. Holding land and status from the king in exchange for military service supplied the formula for being a Macedonian citizen: Both Persians and Macedonians did that. Alexander's policies were in fact no different from Philip's, only on a grander scale. The call to make common cause (*koinonia*) was a pragmatic rather than an idealistic goal, for that was the only way to control so vast an empire.

As with so many things about Alexander, the modern debate reflects the questions from antiquity itself. After Alexander's death, when his Successors (*Diadochoi*) eventually came into their own kingdoms, all but one of them put aside their Persian wives and abandoned any policy of fusion. And Alexander himself was conflicted about it. He continued with his plans to send the 10,000 veterans home. They were ordered to leave their native wives and children behind in Alexander's care, in order to prevent problems back in Macedonia where these men already had wives. But Alexander promised that the sons of these men by their native wives would receive a Macedonian upbringing, "with particular attention to their military training." These amounted to 10,000 men, who were destined for the phalanx. As for the veterans, they were each given a talent of silver, the equivalent of $1 million, as a mustering-out bonus, and left for home under the command of Craterus.

The Last Days

Shortly following the Banquet at Opis, to escape the heat in the plains, Alexander moved the court to the traditional Persian summer palace at Ecbatana (modern Hamadan). Here he put on a set of lavish games in honor of Dionysus, involving both athletic games and *mousika*, literary and musical competitions. In all likelihood, this was an extension to the entire army of the concept of reconciliation that had been the theme at Opis. Some 3000 professionals were brought in from Greece to make these competitions truly spectacular.

During the course of the games and the feasting, Hephaistion fell ill and languished for a week. He seemed to be recovering, and then suffered a sudden relapse and died. Alexander was summoned from the games, but Hephaistion was already dead. Alexander's grief was inconsolable, and he even had the physician attending Hephaistion executed. The king began planning a set of elaborate funeral games to rival Achilles' games for Patroclus in the *Iliad* and which would use the same 3000 professionals hired for the Dionysiac games in Ecbatana. Preparations were detailed and lengthy. The body was escorted

Parade Shield from Tomb II at Vergina. The shield was made from ivory and faience, on a wooden frame, and used for ceremonial purposes only, as it was too delicate to be used in combat. If, as some scholars believe, this is the tomb of Philip III Arrhidaeus (Alexander's brother), then this shield was most likely an artifact of Alexander himself. The other possibility is that it belonged to Philip II (Alexander's father). (Photograph by Winthrop Lindsay Adams, taken at the archaeological site at Vergina.)

to Babylon, where the funeral rites were carried out in the next spring. The monument alone would cost more than 10,000 talents.

Part of this extravagance was undeniably grief, but part was Homeric propaganda and tremendous self-indulgence. One might well ask "Why?" The Homeric concept of the hero, which formed so much of Alexander's image of himself, was defined by *arete,* the Greek term meaning excellence or prowess. It was the capacity to do all things with great flare or panache, whether it was fighting, drinking, or mourning. Everything was outsized, a grand gesture. In a letter to Aristotle, Alexander had once stated that he would rather "excel in knowledge and *arete* than in my power." Indeed, this has enduring meaning for modern Greeks and the word *arete* was a logo used by them for the Olympic games in Athens in 2004. The grief and funeral games for Hephaistion fit that image of *arete*.

But the grief went further than Homeric imitation. In the ancient Greek tradition of the *erastes,* the "beloved," Alexander and Hephaistion were most likely lovers. The question of Alexander's sexuality is a modern, not an ancient one. There was no such thing as sexual orientation, in the modern sense of the term, for the ancient Greeks. One took one's pleasure where one found it. To think in "homosexual," "heterosexual," or "bisexual" terms would be unintelligible to a Greek, who could best be commonly described as "omnisexual," if one had to apply a modern term. If Alexander had a romantic relationship with Hephaistion, he also had relationships with at least four women: his three wives, Roxane, Stateira, and Parysatis, and a mistress, Barsine, the widow of Memnon of Rhodes. His father, Philip II, had seven wives of varying status, innumerable mistresses, and occasional youthful male lovers.

The point is that sex in and of itself held no particular guilt for the Greeks and was irrelevant to their other behavior. As with Alexander and deification, it is potentially a problem only for modern society. It was a problem for the Greeks if the relationship was destructive or addictive or turned them from their duty to family and state. This applied equally to an obsessive heterosexual relationship as it did to a homosexual one. No sexual relationship of any kind ever distracted Alexander from his purpose. But on this occasion, it explains the depth of his grief.

Nor were the memorials for Hephaistion the only monuments planned. They were part of an immense building program which included a pyramid for Philip, conveniently evoking the images of both Philip and Zeus Ammon, and seven more temples and shrines equaling at least another 10,000 talents were planned. None of them, nor the monument to Hephaistion, was ever built, as all these projects were cancelled by Alexander's death.

As autumn of 324 B.C.E. came on, Alexander took out some of his grief and anger on what was to be his last campaign. A hill tribe, the Cossaeans, in the Zagros Mountains southwest of Ecbatana had for generations been paid off by the Persians, bribed into not raiding the caravan routes. Alexander took this occasion to end the practice. In a five-week campaign he literally wiped out the entire tribe, raising another charge of ethnic cleansing.

Throughout the winter and spring of 323 B.C.E., more plans were made. A fleet was ordered built to explore the Caspian Sea; plans were made for a campaign against Scythia, the modern-day area of the central Asian republics of the former Soviet Union; and the conquest of Arabia was contemplated. Further possibilities included the conquest of North Africa and Carthage, of Sicily, and southern Italy where his uncle Alexander of Epirus had been killed in 330 B.C.E.. As with his architectural plans, none of this would be carried out. They are, in fact, the sign of a restless mind probably bored with the routine of government.

Still, government had to be conducted. In the spring, Alexander returned to Babylon. Complaints from the Greek states had reached him that Antipater had been too tightly controlling them with pro-Macedonian parties and mercenary garrisons. Alexander had sent for Antipater to come and explain himself, though Alexander knew full well that these measures had been used after the battle at Megapolis, and had to be used. Alexander had drawn out from home some 60,000 Macedonians in the original force and reinforcements over the years. Antipater did not have enough Macedonians left to hold Greece by himself, as events were to prove after Alexander's death. Craterus was already on his way back to Macedonia with the 10,000 veterans and orders to replace Antipater as general for Europe. For the meantime, Antipater sent his son Cassander to speak for him.

It was an unfortunate choice. Cassander and Alexander had a deep antipathy for one another dating back to their childhood. Further, Cassander had not been on the expedition. When he saw some Persians performing *proskynesis,* ritual obeisance to the Great King, he burst out laughing. Alexander lost his temper and dashed Cassander's head against the wall. It was only the latest incident of Alexander's growing problem with self-control. Again interpretations of this range from an example of Lord Acton's axiom that "If power corrupts, then absolute power corrupts absolutely," to the fact Alexander had not been feeling well for some time. The points are not mutually exclusive and are more useful in demonstrating again that people make of Alexander almost anything they want.

On May 29, Alexander attended a banquet in Babylon, following which he contracted a fever. Over the course of the next week, the illness worsened. By June 6, he could barely speak, and gave his signet ring to Perdikkas, who had been

exercising the office of Chiliarch after Hephaistion's death, although he did not have the title.
As word got out to the army that Alexander was
gravely ill, his old veterans clamored to see him.
They were allowed to pass through his resting
place. By this time, Alexander could no longer
speak, but now and again raised a hand to an
old comrade here or there. He died in the early
morning of June 10, less than two months shy of
his thirty-third birthday.

Five years later, in the midst of the wars to
control the empire, Olympias would claim that
Alexander was poisoned by Cassander and his
brothers. It was part of a propaganda campaign
to justify her killing of a hundred of Cassander's
friends and taking over the government. No suspicion had been raised at the time, and the details of the plot are preposterous: That Aristotle
concocted the poison, which was so strong it
could only be contained in the hoof of a mule; and
that it was administered by Cassander's brothers,
who were the cupbearer and food taster to the
king during the period of his illness. The story
was dismissed in antiquity, but still has some
currency among modern historians interested in
conspiracy theory, on the basis of the history of
all too real intrigues at the Macedonian court. A
poison as strong as claimed here would have
killed immediately, and in any event, protracted

poisoning in small doses was inherently too risky. Alexander had never fully recovered from the punctured lung in India; the sources refer to his not feeling well for some months before returning to Babylon. Frequently the simplest explanation is the best: With his physical and psychological resistance down, he contracted a fever in an area noted for such things and succumbed naturally. But even in death, Alexander remains surrounded by controversy.

The Classical Legacy of Alexander

In the end, Alexander left behind more questions than he had resolved, for he left no heir. Nor had he established any permanent structure for the empire. Even Perdikkas, who held Alexander's signet ring, was not officially the Chiliarch. Within days, out of necessity, an officers' council was called, which confirmed Perdikkas as Chiliarch and all standing orders. Roxane was pregnant, and the popular sentiment was to await the outcome of that pregnancy rather than name a king. But the phalanx took matters into its own hands and demanded that the sole remaining son of Philip, Arrhidaeus, be named king and assaulted the headquarters to make their point.

A compromise was reached, which acknowledged Arrhidaeus as Philip III, renamed to make the connection clear, but allowed for a joint kingship if Roxane bore a son. This she did a few months later, naming him Alexander IV Aegis, to reflect his being born "under the shield." Since Philip III Arrhidaeus was mentally incompetent (the exact nature of which is unknown) and Alexander IV an infant, a regency under Perdikkas was established jointly for the kings. A new round of satrapal appointments was made, in which Ptolemy received Egypt.

Back in Greece, Athens and the poleis rose against Antipater in Macedon, as the League of Corinth had dissolved with the death of Alexander. The situation would be restored by Craterus and the returning 10,000 veterans, but the Lamian War opened a struggle over the nature and existence of the empire itself. One group, composed of different states or generals at different times each with their own motives, fought to break up imperial control and stake claims to their own territories. Another, again composed of differing factions at different times for differing reasons, fought to maintain imperial authority, at first in the name of the kings and then for their own ambitions. These constituted the Wars of the Diadochoi, the successors to Alexander, which lasted until 280 B.C.E. The immediate legacy of Alexander was that his empire fell apart.

During the course of those wars, the Argead royal house was wiped out, and three kingdoms emerged from the numerous factions that began this "Game of Empire": the Antigonid royal house, which controlled Macedonia and most of Greece; the Ptolemaic royal house, which controlled Egypt and many of the Greek islands and ports; and the Seleucid royal house, which controlled Asia Minor, Mesopotamia, and ostensibly most of Iran. A balance of power emerged among these three kingdoms, each of which had its advantages. The Seleucids controlled the largest area and population. Further, Seleucus remained married to his Iranian wife, Apama, and their son, Antiochus, would succeed him on the throne. Seleucus believed in Alexander's policy of fusion. It was into his phalanx that the Iranian sons of the Macedonian veterans and the Macedonian-trained Persian Cardaces were incorporated. They formed a recognized group of Macedonians, who were the central support of the dynasty and grew in number over the years, a distinct legacy of Alexander's policy. The Seleucids had the largest army of the three powers, but also a vast territory to control and only about 30,000 in their Macedonian phalanx.

Ptolemy, in Egypt, rejected Alexander's ideas about integrating the Macedonians with the native population. Instead, he separated his two *personae:* He was a basileus (king) to his Greco-Macedonians, with all of the traditional court ritual (and no substance); but he was Pharaoh to his Egyptians, again with all of that ritual kept separately. To the average Egyptian, the ruler was as he had always been: portrayed in the traditional manner on the monuments, carrying the traditional five names of the Pharaoh on the documents, maintaining all of the religious institutions of the ancient kingdom. Manetho, an Egyptian priest, wrote a history of Egypt for Ptolemy, identifying thirty dynasties, the Ptolemies being the XXX, which is still used as the historical division of ancient Egypt to this day. The Ptolemies ruled from Alexandria, and several other Greek cities were established in Egypt, but they were only a thin veneer over the native population. The Ptolemies' influence came from their immense wealth.

The Antigonids controlled the Macedonian homeland and Greece, but it was a much-depopulated region. Greeks and Macedonians burst out of the Aegean in a flood of emigration. They settled into the two dozen cities in Afghanistan, which ultimately formed the Greek Kingdom of Bactria that lasted until 30 B.C.E. Others went into the eighty Greek foundations in Asia Minor and Mesopotamia, some new cities and others, long-existing ones refounded formally to reinforce their new identities as Greek cities. The population of Macedonia dropped from about 800,000 to about 250,000. Greece likewise was affected. Within a century, Athens chose to become a neutral state and opted out of politics altogether. It became a university town, the seat of Plato's Academy, Aristotle's Lyceum, and the three great Hellenistic philosophic schools: Epicureanism, Cyncism, and Stoicism. By the first century B.C.E. Athens was a city of about 30,000. But however reduced the Antigonids and the Greek homeland might be, they maintained the traditions of Philip and Alexander, and man for man, they had the best army in the East.

This world is the Hellenistic world, Alexander's direct legacy. It saw Greek culture spread to the Himalayas in the East, but equally was the conduit for Greek culture to the West. For those Greeks who had left the world of the Polis, where they had extended families and were bound to all by blood and tradition in a largely agricultural community, it was a new world indeed. It was one in which they had only their nuclear family and settled into big cities where most people did not speak Greek. It was a world of immigrants. A language emerged, based on old Attic Greek, which became the common language of trade, science, philosophy, and literature: Koine [or "Common"] Greek. Ironically, in Greece itself, this broke down the perceived ethnic differences between Greeks and Macedonians. Those differences were already indistinguishable to the peoples of the Near East and would become so for the Romans as well. This is another legacy of Alexander: a Greek cultural union impossible before. The Greek language was spoken by Greeks and Near Eastern natives alike and is the language in which the *New Testament* is written.

Despite the political fracturing of the old Persian Empire, the economic aspects of Persian rule remained intact: roads, trade routes, unified systems of coinage, weights, and measures. Nothing hindered trade, which indeed was greatly expanded into the markets of Greece. Just as readily, markets for Greek goods now existed as far away as Afghanistan and India. Through the Greek world as entrepreneurs, especially Ptolemaic Egypt, Rhodes and Pergamum, they even expanded to the Romans and the West. This too was a legacy of Alexander.

For the Greeks in the hot and dusty Near East, no longer directly connected to their homeland and culture, becoming reconnected was all important. The Hellenistic philosophic schools mentioned earlier all had this as their central theme: how to reconnect your soul to a sense of belonging to the Cosmos. Literature extolled the Heroic Greek past (our copies of Homer ultimately date back to Alexandrian versions); idyllic

poetry which sang the praises of a simple country life to a people living in vast cities; and art
which replicated in growing romantic style the
myths, stories, and history of the past. All this
the Hellenistic East passed directly on to Rome,
another legacy of Alexander.

Most of all, however, in the minds of the
rulers of the three kingdoms was the fact that
Alexander had been ruler of a united empire.
The balance of power would only be temporary,
and one of them would emerge to reestablish
that empire, to be the new Alexander. Ptolemy,
as a sign of that, even hijacked Alexander's funeral cortege on the way back to Macedonia and
set up Alexander's sarcophagus in a special funer-
ary temple, the Sema, in Alexandria. Alexander's
coin portraits continued to be struck. Histories
from his leading commanders were written and
circulated and the *Royal Journals* published. The
Alexander Romance emerged, and was, for all
intents and purposes, the first historical novel,
which celebrated his many feats. His name and
the possibilities that name evoked remained. As
it turned out, the Romans raided the "Game of
Empire" and one by one destroyed the Hellenistic
kingdoms. The Romans took them over as
provinces; first Macedonia in the second century,
then Seleucid Syria in the first century B.C.E.
The last Ptolemaic ruler, Cleopatra VII, tried to

use Marc Antony's Roman legions to establish a new version of Alexander's empire in the last episodes of the Roman civil wars. Augustus brought an end to Cleopatra and the Ptolemaic kingdom in 30 B.C.E.

By this point, the idea of Alexander and the legacy of his conquests had already been transferred, along with Hellenistic culture, to Rome. Caesar as a praetorian governor in Spain, on seeing a portrait of Alexander, lamented that he was in his late thirties and had yet to do any great thing, while at a younger age Alexander had already conquered the world. Other Roman emperors would emulate Alexander, including Trajan who actually set out in Alexander's footsteps. And it was the Romans who gave Alexander the title of "Magnus," the Great. If Alexander's legacy went no further, it would still be remarkable. But in fact it did; it was a global legacy, in some ways mirroring the events in the classical world, and in others providing a new cast to things.

The World Legacy of Alexander

In the East, especially along the Indus, Alexander's life and death left things in as much turmoil as in the eastern Mediterranean. His attempts to leave a stable satrapal government there collapsed as soon as he left, which had prompted Nearchus' early departure with the fleet in 325 B.C.E..

Alexander's harsh methods and widespread destruction had stirred up a hornet's nest. Soon after his death, an adventurer from the Ganges, Chandragupta, seized control of the Nanda kingdom of Magadha in Bihar (India Proper). With the help of a ruler presumed to be Porus, he expanded into the Indus valley and established the Mauryan Empire. To a large extent, Chandragupta used the Greek mercenaries and Macedonians left behind (called "Yavana" in the local dialect) as the core of his army, a physical legacy of Alexander. Chandragupta wound up stabilizing the area, but not in the way Alexander had expected. Nevertheless, as such identifiable Greek communities and inscriptions can be found in the region over the course of the next 300 years.

Chandragupta (Sandracottus to the Greeks and Romans) ruled for almost thirty years. In 305 B.C.E., recognizing his inability to hold the three satrapies Alexander had set up for the Sind, Seleucus met with Chandragupta and negotiated a settlement. A marriage alliance was made, and Seleucus Nicator, the founder of the Seleucid monarchy, gave up his claims in exchange for 500 Indian war elephants and the breeding stock to maintain them. Some eight years later Chandrgupta became a Jain convert and followed his guru into obscurity, but his empire and its Greek communities lived on. His grandson, Asoka, became a Buddhist convert and sent missionaries to the Greek communities, especially along the frontier. Asoka's father, Bindusura, had previously sent to the Seleucids asking for fig trees and a Sophist, by which he meant a Greek philosopher. The latter had to be declined because the Seleucids said they did not control the source for Sophists: Athens.

An interesting cultural exchange, nevertheless, took place. Arrian makes it clear that Seleucus in particular, and the Macedonians in general, had been fascinated by what they called the gymnosophists, the naked wise men of India: the fakirs and gurus who likewise fascinated the Europeans of a later age. Some of these gymnosophists accompanied the expedition back to Persia. And other interactions may have taken place. The Buddhists and Jainists already shared a central tenet with Diogenes of Sinope and the Cynic Philosophical School, which was asceticism. By rejecting the material world, Diogenes had felt that one could free the soul of encumbrances and thereby achieve a oneness with the Cosmos. By the third century B.C.E., Cynic philosophers felt themselves *kosmopolites,* "citizens of the world," and unattached to any one place. They were wanderers, identified in the Hellenistic East by their hiking staff and the beggar's wallet, reminiscent of the Buddhist monks in the East. The governmental requests for exchange may have been impossible, but personal ones were not.

Along the Indus itself other cultural interactions were evident. The Greek communities helped to produce a distinctive phase of Indian art, called the "Ghandaran." Initially, this manifested itself in decorative art and sculpture with clear Hellenic origins. By long tradition in India, Buddha had only been represented in aniconic form, as the Wheel of Law, or an empty throne, or a footprint. The earliest representations of Buddha in human form are Ghandaran, and have a distinctive Greek tone. In particular, Buddha does not have a shaved head, but full hair, and is represented in imitation of royal portraiture. The original model is probably from Alexander portraiture (or alternately Apollo), an unexpected legacy. And there are clear references to Buddhist stupas (shrines) and Jainist traditions in Alexander sources for this period, particularly in Pompeius Trogus, which showed that knowledge of these things went both ways. In the last century, the archaeologist Sir Aurel Stein even followed Alexander's track to the Indus, while seeking out the earliest line of Buddhist shrines that lay along the same line.

Asoka set up a series of giant rock inscriptions in Aramaic and Greek, as well as Sanskrit, to mark his Buddhist missionary efforts to the Greeks on his frontiers. Later inscriptions make it clear that those communities became part of Asoka's domain. But by that point a Greek state had emerged in Bactria (modern Afghanistan) just beyond the Mauryan empire, which stretched from the Khyber Pass up to the Oxus River, including the city that forms the great ruins at Ai Khanoum, probably Alexandria Oxiana, another legacy of Alexander. This kingdom emerged from the two dozen Greek settlements Alexander had left there in the wake of the guerilla war. They established their independence from the Seleucids and maintained it after the Parthians had conquered the Iranian plateau (briefly in the third century and permanently in the second century B.C.E.).

A succession of some forty Greek kings controlled the area over the next three centuries. Eventually, they succumbed to the pressure of the Scythians and other nomads. A late second century Chinese diplomat found the area teeming with Yueh-Chi and Hiung Nu (Huns), and the last of the Greek kings retreated to the area around modern Kandahar, another Alexandrian foundation. It was destroyed in the same year that Ptolemaic Egypt fell to the Romans, 30 B.C.E. But even to this day there are local Pashtun tribesmen on both sides of the Khyber Pass who claim descent from Alexander, or one or another of his generals, and horses that are said to be descended from Bucephalus.

In one way or another, many people claimed Alexander's legacy, even the Persians. Some of these traditions are unique, while others relate in one way or another to the *Greek Alexander Romance,* or the so-called Pseudo-Callisthenes. This was essentially a work of historical fiction written in the third century B.C.E., which was conveniently (though incorrectly) attributed to Callisthenes, Aristotle's nephew and Alexander's propagandist. It survives in some eighty Greek versions alone, which blend tales of Alexander's exploits with imaginary correspondence. It was enormously popular, as witnessed by the number of versions that have come down over the centuries. More important, major versions of the Romance were also written in Armenian, Coptic, and Syriac, and elements showed up in Ethiopian, Hebrew, and Persian literature.

The Persian traditions are the most varied and include hostile portraits from Zoroastrian sources. Here Alexander is identified as "The Accursed," urged on by evil spirits and creating chaos. The burning of Persepolis and the destruction of sacred texts are the chief examples of this, but essentially Alexander is seen as a creature of the God of Darkness, Ahriman. The remaining three traditions all actually lay claim to Alexander. One line of these comes through the *Koran* as Iskander Dhul-Qarnein (Alexander, "Lord of the Two Horns"), in which Alexander is a chosen servant of Allah. The reference is to the rams-head coin portrait of Alexander that iconographically refers to Zeus-Ammon. But this was also the most common coin type for Alexander, which was circulated widely and thus the portrait most people saw. The popular identification of Alexander as two-horned, then, was intended to identify him with a common portrait rather than as a religious reference to pagan Egypt. The Persians would hold these images in common with their fellow Moslems.

But equally, Alexander is a central part in the work of two of the great medieval Persian poets, Firdawsi and Nizameh. Firdawsi wrote an epic poem, the *Shahnameh* or "Book of Kings," in the eleventh century C.E. in which the father of Alexander was Darab, briefly married to a daughter of Philip. Though she is already pregnant, Darab returns her to her father, and in Macedonia she bears Alexander. Darab then sires another son in Persia, Darius, and the two are destined to fight for the throne. Alexander, thus, is the older son, who restores his rightful rule. The twelfth-century poet Nizameh, in the *Iskandernameh* or "Book of Alexander," tells a similar tale, but adds fabulous deeds to it largely derived from the *Alexander Romance* as well as calling Alexander by his nickname from the *Koran,* Dhul-Qarnein, tying together all three traditions. For both poets, then, Alexander is actually a Persian and thus one of their own.

Among the most interesting lines of traditions is the Arabic one. In the *Koran,* Alexander is one of the few men chosen by Allah for a divine mission: to cast down the idols of unbelievers. He is also an exemplar of the ideal king who establishes just laws, punishes the guilty, is kind to the righteous, and one who recognizes his own shortcomings, and is thus humble before God. Admittedly, it is somewhat harder to recognize the historical Alexander in this, but not the "idea" of Alexander. He becomes the symbol of the "ideal" ruler, just as in the West he became the symbol of the ideal conqueror. Last, it is Alexander who locks Gog and Magog up behind iron gates until the end of the world, tying him to Jewish traditions as well.

There is also a historical tradition of Alexander in Arabic which can be seen in the works of the first great Arab historians: al-Dinawari, al-Ya'qubi, and al-Tabari. For the most part, these blend the *Alexander Romance* with the Koranic tradition. They were widely read and equally popularized Alexander, making him the predecessor of the caliphs. The Arabic Iskander, thus, becomes a legendary figure who is incorporated into local Islamic traditions as far away as China and Malaysia, where he is part of royal genealogies. Most common of all, as Iskander, Alexander shows up even in the *Tales of the Thousand Nights and the One Night.*

Alexander had already become a religious hero in the Jewish tradition when the *Koran* was written, and that is the probable conduit into the Arabic tradition for Alexander. Part of this is a Hebrew version of the *Alexander Romance,* but on three occasions Alexander becomes Jewish. In the first of these, he visits Jerusalem and is met by the High Priest, (a position and title) in whom he recognizes a figure that had come to Alexander in a dream, and acknowledges Jehovah. The second time is before the Gates of Paradise, and the third, when seeking the Land of the Blest, the Children of Moses.

The image of Alexander as an ideal king is here as well. He does homage to God in Jerusalem, permits the observance of the law, and encourages the Jews to settle in Alexandria (in Egypt) where they are accorded the same privileges as the Greeks. Thus, Alexander begins the Great Jewish Diaspora. In fact, the Ptolemies did encourage this. Crack Jewish mercenaries were used throughout Egypt, especially at Elephantine (Aswan), and as administrators in the bureaucracy.

A whole quarter of Alexandria (the "Delta" section) was dedicated to the Jewish community. It produced such philosophers as Philo, and Jewish scholars there translated the *Torah, Prophets* and *Writings (TANAK)* into Greek as *The Septuagint.*

Older Biblical traditions were reinterpreted in light of Alexander. In the prophecies from the Book of Daniel, Alexander becomes the third king who destroys harsh Persian rule and is symbolized by a leopard with four heads and four wings. A later vision of Daniel sees Alexander as a he-goat with one horn between his eyes. Finally, Alexander again becomes the means by which the hordes of Gog and Magog are locked up behind the Iron Gates of Debend until the end of world. There are virtually identical Syrian Christian and Ethiopian Christian versions of these, equally seeing Alexander as a servant of God, and locking up Gog and Magog until the end of the millennial kingdom.

Thus, the popular image of Alexander became part of the fabric of cultures stretching from western China and Southeast Asia to the eastern Mediterranean. The skeins of these traditions are in popular culture and literature, folklore and religion. In all these, Alexander becomes an ideal, and the various traditions wind up doing just what the historians of Alexander have done: making of Alexander whatever they will.

The same is true in the medieval and modern western tradition. Alexander shows up in French and German romance literature, a common subject of poetry. More frequently Alexander has a religious message to deliver and is used in sermons and moral tales to the same effect as he was used in Islam, Judaism, and eastern Christianity. Much of this, as with the eastern tradition, was derived from the *Alexander Romance*. All were intended to teach a lesson: Alexander and the Wonderstone; Alexander and the Wheel of Fortune; Alexander and the Celestial Journey; Alexander and the Diving Bell. They are represented in art and song as well. In its own way, this Alexander legacy unites East and West in its traditions and in a far more concrete way than Alexander's life did. It made it a world legacy.

Epilogue

In the end, we now have the same problem with which we set out in this study. What do you make of Alexander the Great and his legacy?

According to Plutarch, Alexander "did not desire pleasure or even wealth, but rather excellence [*arete*] and glory" (Alex. 5.3). As it turned out, Alexander achieved fabulous wealth, overindulged in pleasure, and left a legacy of glory that lasts to this day in popular culture. But the key to Alexander is *arete*. The definition of that Homeric heroic tradition was best expressed in the *Iliad* by Glaucus, who was one of the Trojan heroes, ironically, as "to be the best, and to hold my head above the others" (6. 208). As stated before, *arete* was the aristocratic ability to do all things greatly, with panache.

Alexander never doubted his destiny and certainly achieved his goals as stated by Plutarch.

Everything he did was outsized, greater than life, exhibiting *arete*. This applies to both his achievements and his failures, his virtues and his vices. It is a commonplace of historians to point to this path as one of killing, plunder, and destruction. If so, it was a well-trod path, following Persians, Chaldaeans, Assyrians, Hittites, and Egyptians stretching ever further back into history. For that matter, the Romans, Byzantines, and Arabs would carry it forward, with Alexander in no small part as an exemplar. In the same vein Wellington would refer to Napoleon as "the Great Thief of Europe." In any event, to judge Alexander by any other standards but those of his own time is idle, and there is more than enough there already to provide discussion.

More pointedly, many modern Alexander historians have belittled his legacy by pointing out that his achievements in conquest were short lived and his long-term legacies (culturally) were totally unintended. At the other end of the spectrum, the late N. G. L. Hammond once made the point that: "Our modern age is marked, to cite the words of Thomas Carlyle, 'by a disbelief in great men' because our age has so signally failed to produce statesmen and leaders of such stature." There is no remedy for this problem, which lies both in the historians who write on Alexander and in Alexander himself. All one can do is look at the sources themselves.

There is no doubt that Alexander's path was strewn with destruction and death. Detractors can and do point to how Alexander dealt with native peoples. The fate of the populations of Halicarnassus, Tyre, and Gaza in Alexander's sieges stand as examples of that, as we have seen. So too does the brutality we saw in the Afghan and Indian campaigns and Alexander's final military action in the complete destruction of the Cossaean hill tribe in the Zagros Mountains, which amounted to genocide. For this reason, as well as the burning of Persepolis, the Zoroastrian tradition (as noted in the last chapter) viewed Alexander as the "Accursed" and the bringer of chaos.

But one could argue that these actions were not ethnically based. Alexander was equally brutal with Thebes and Miletus, which were Greek cities; and he was as murderous to Greek mercenaries as to Zagros Mountain tribesmen. If there are more examples of this among native peoples in the Near East, it is because Alexander spent most of his time outside of Greece campaigning in Asia; he had more opportunity there. Of course, one could maintain that all this shows is that Alexander was an equal opportunity oppressor. Fortunately, that is not all there is.

If the people of Halicarnassus, Tyre, and Gaza saw Alexander as a destroyer, the Judaeans, Egyptians, and Babylonians saw him as a liberator from Persian oppression. Alexander ended Persian cultural and religious persecution, restored the ancient worship, and enforced tolerance. Egyptian gods and customs were celebrated; Persian restrictions and taxes on Judaism (according to Jewish tradition) were lifted; Babylonian temples and worship were restored. And he did the same for the Greeks of Asia Minor, ending Persian oppression and restoring democracy. These were hardly unintentional but rather deliberate policies of Alexander. The Hellenistic age for the most part showed that this policy continued to last at least until the mid-second century B.C.E., hardly short lived.

While Alexander was in the process of conducting a brutal guerilla war in Afghanistan, he was also restoring Iranian chieftains and officials to civil governance in the satrapies throughout Iran proper. At the same time, he was incorporating Iranian levies into his army, particularly the cavalry. He maintained Persian court ritual and custom, against considerable opposition from his own Macedonians. He tried to rule the Persians as they were accustomed to being ruled, demonstrating a genuine concern for native sensibilities.

Alexander encouraged a mixing of Persian and Macedonian culture. He married according to Persian fashion and ultimately took three Persian princesses as brides. One of them, Roxane, bore him two sons: Herakles, who died in infancy in India, and his ultimate heir Alexander IV, born after Alexander the Great's death. In the same vein, with his urging, some eighty of Alexander's Companions and 10,000 of his men also married Iranian women. Historians can doubt, and have doubted, the altruistic and idealistic interpretation of this as a union of "East and West," but that Alexander's intention was the creation of a practical ruling class isn't really open to interpretation; the marriages took place for a reason. At the feast at Opis following the "mutiny," Alexander called on both Persians and Macedonians to live in *homonoia* (equality) and make *koinonia* (common cause) under his reign. The primary call was to the Macedonians, who were the most resistant to the idea, but it still reflects Alexander's thoughts on his policy.

The practical applications of that policy can be seen in Alexander integrating the elite Persian cavalry units directly into the Companions, not as separate entities. Equally, he ordered the training of 30,000 Persian Cardaces in the Macedonian fashion, equipped with Macedonian arms, and ordered their incorporation directly into the phalanx. This was, in part, the reason for the mutiny at Opis, but Alexander kept the Cardaces afterwards. The children by native women of the 10,000 veterans Alexander sent home were to be trained and educated as Macedonians, guaranteed by a personal promise by Alexander. Altogether these acts are clearly a comprehensive imperial policy, with many different manifestations, rather than a mere aberration to be dismissed. Alexander may not have wanted to unite the world, but he certainly did his best to unite the peoples who controlled his empire, a legacy carried on by Seleucus and his descendants for more than 200 years.

If Alexander destroyed cities such as Halicarnassus, Tyre, and Gaza, he rebuilt them as well, and many more. Following the Macedonian tradition, these new foundations were invariably of mixed populations: Greco-Macedonian and the local natives. In many cases these were re-foundations of existing towns, in others new cities altogether. Regardless, the conscious creation of Greek styled poleis in Anatolia, Egypt, Mesopotamia, Persia, Afghanistan, and India was practical as well as altruistic. It did have the effect of spreading Greek culture by Alexander, but also of holding territory for him and as a means of incorporating the natives into the Macedonian structure as participants, not just subjects.

This is exactly what Philip II had done in creating a Macedonian state to begin with and clearly reflects Alexander's intention to create his imperial state. Alexander's death truncated the creation of that imperial state, but the fact that he established a Greek presence in Afghanistan and India that lasted 300 years is also clear. Three centuries is hardly short lived, and one is constrained to point out that it was longer than the existence so far of the United States as a sovereign nation.

But to balance his achievements, Alexander's failures were great as well. First, they were accomplished at a terrible price in bloodshed on the part of the conquered, and even the ancient sources such as Arrian remark that this was excessively so. It drained human resources from and ultimately crippled Macedonia and the Greek homeland; and though this was certainly unintentional, it was equally real. Though Alexander had some general ideas about cultural integration, and some practical ones on personal, urban, and military levels, he failed utterly to create a government for the empire as a whole, the old Persian Empire, Greece and Macedonia. He himself arrested or executed half of his own satrapal appointments within the old Persian area, and his chief financial minister, Harpalus, absconded with embezzled funds. Even what administration he did try failed. Likewise, his attempts to create a stable Greece, built on Philip's foundation of the League of Corinth, did not last beyond word of his death. Indeed, Alexander's Exiles' Decree may very likely have aggravated it.

He conquered a great empire, but failed to provide for any transition in the event of his death. One might argue that Alexander's death was somewhat unexpected, but for a commander who led his troops personally in even the most difficult of circumstances, early and sudden death must be viewed as likely. Parmenio and Antipater had warned of it even before the expedition began, and Alexander had been wounded many times. The failure to make those provisions saw his achievements sundered within a few years of Alexander's death, at first by Greek uprisings in both Greece proper and Afghanistan, and then among his own generals.

This penchant to do all things greatly is found on a personal level with Alexander as well. His courage and fighting ability were self-evident, but so too was the rashness he showed at the Battle of the Granicus. Alexander had an uncanny tactical genius and tremendous charisma as seen at Issus, Gaugamela, and the Hyphasis, but he frequently also demonstrated a total lack of strategic thinking. He failed to pursue Darius after the Battle of Issus; he all but ignored the revolt of Agis in Greece; and he conducted the endless campaigns in central Asia with only the thought of continuing as the main purpose, until his army forced him to turn back. That charisma could get his men to do things even they didn't dream they could do, but he also used it to lead them on the awful march back through the Makran desert.

Strong emotion was a hallmark of Alexander's character, demonstrated in his devotion to his friends, but also leading into all sorts of excesses. A good example is the continual resurfacing of a *pothos* to see exotic places such as the Danube, the Oasis of Siwah, the Jaxartes River, 'Ocean' in India, or the crossing of the Makran Desert just because they were there. That same emotion also saw him singlemindedly seek the deaths of Parmenio and Philotas, and kill Kleitos the Black with his own hands. Then he mourned almost inconsolably over what he had done. Again, part of this reflects Alexander's Homeric self-image (his *arete*), as in the grand gestures of his funeral rites for Hephaistion. Alexander found it increasingly difficult to control his temper, and he showed that to both nobles such as Cassander and to the army at the mutiny at Opis.

These all express the original dichotomy in understanding Alexander, among both his contemporaries and those who came after who either romanticized Alexander or demonized him.

Though larger than life, Alexander was a complex individual as all humans are complex individuals. His personal failings have a way of humanizing him, and removing him from the category of a monolithic statue. He becomes a real character. And that as much as his achievements is what has drawn people to study Alexander both as a historical figure and as a personality in popular culture. The great Roman historian Theodor Mommsen once wrote, "Those who have lived through historical events, as I have, begin to see that history is neither written nor made without love or hate." That is certainly true of Alexander the Great.

A Note on the Sources

Among the things that are important for historians to know about any subject in which they are interested is how we know what we know about that topic. In the case of Alexander, we are dealing with a topic that is 2300 years old. Indeed, the study of the sources for Alexander is a major subject in itself for which the Germans even invented a term: *Alexanderquellenforschungsgeschichte* (a complicated word meaning the "History of Alexander Sources Studies"). The sources for all historical studies are divided into "primary" and "secondary" sources, though in ancient history, the latter is also divided into "ancient" and "modern" secondary sources.

A primary source is anything contemporary to an event or series of events, in this case the life of Alexander. For the most part these are literary sources: eyewitness accounts, memoirs, reports, laws, inscriptions, and even graffiti. But primary sources can also be artifacts discovered by archaeology: pottery, armor, the contents of tombs, the remains of buildings and roads, the wrecks of ships, coins, and trade items. In many cases, these artifacts inform the narrative sources, challenging or confirming what the author has to say.

A secondary source, whether a few years later or a couple of thousand years later, is anything written *after* the event by someone who did not witness the events. In the case of Alexander, the closest surviving narrative source was written some three centuries after the events of his life. In modern terms, since the eighteenth century C.E., Alexander has been a constant theme and matter of interest. The bibliography on Alexander in the modern era is arguably larger than that for any other secular figure from antiquity.

The Primary Literary Sources

There were, in fact, numerous written contemporary sources for Alexander and his campaigns that survived for hundreds of years. Though most of these are lost to us today, many of the ancient secondary writers had access to them. In terms of artifacts, there are likewise thousands of items which have survived to this day: coins; inscriptions (laws, decrees, even open letters set in stone); arms and armor; sculptures; pottery and even paintings such as frescoes (paintings executed in plaster on walls). But our main concern is with literary sources.

To begin with, Alexander ordered a journal kept and had a staff to keep it up to date. This was the *Ephemerides* (or the *Royal Journal* or "Daybook"). It contained the full record of the king's actions, orders issued, religious sacrifices held, and pronouncements by the king, correspondence, and reports received. This record was kept by a Greek subject of Alexander, Eumenes of Cardia (a town in the Hellespont), who was one of his Hetairoi. Eumenes was the *archigrammateus*, or chief secretary, and had a staff working under him. There were probably several working copies of the *Royal Journal* kept, but only one official copy.

Normally, this would have been sent back to the royal archives in Macedonia (which we know were kept intact as far as the Battle of Pydna in 168 B.C.E., when the Romans took it). But Ptolemy I Soter, Alexander's boyhood friend who became king of Egypt, hijacked the *Ephemerides* at the same time he took Alexander's funeral cortege and brought them both to his capital of Alexandria. Alexander's body was eventually placed in a special memorial, the *Sema*, in the royal enclosure. The *Royal Journal* went into the Library at Alexandria attached to the Museum that Ptolemy founded (arguably the first university). It was quoted extensively by Ptolemy in his own eyewitness history of Alexander's campaigns, and later by Arrian (our best ancient source on Alexander) both when Arrian quoted Ptolemy and in Arrian's own use of the *Journal* directly. There were also two published versions of the *Ephemerides*, one by Strattis of Olynthus (in Macedonia) and Philinus of Akragas (a city on Sicily). However, there is considerable debate about both these versions (how much is genuine and how much fictional), and they only survive today in fragments.

There were a number of other contemporary sources. Callisthenes, Aristotle's nephew, accompanied the expedition into Bactria, where he was implicated in the royal pages' plot. He was imprisoned and died. Up to that point, Callisthenes had been both the official historian and the chief spin-doctor for the expedition, turning out propaganda for Alexander both at home and in the expedition. His *Achievements of Alexander* covered events at least down to Gaugamela.

Cleitarchus, the son of Dinon, an author who wrote on Persia, was an Asia Minor Greek and a contemporary of Alexander. He wrote a *History of Alexander* in twelve books (which means scrolls, equal to about forty of our printed pages each). It is part fact and part fiction, basically a historical novel that did much to sensationalize and romanticize Alexander. Cleitarchus did not accompany the expedition, nor did he have access to its records. It is a good example of a contemporary source *not* necessarily being the best resource.

Chares of Mytiline was the chamberlain (*eisangeleus*) at Alexander's court. His memoirs and writings, *The Histories of Alexander*, were extensive, and Plutarch used him as a source in particular. Our accounts of the *proskynesis* affair and the wedding feast at Susa are largely drawn from him.

Marsyas of Pella grew up with Alexander and served with him among the Royal Pages, and therefore was also a student of Aristotle. Marsyas was the brother of Antigonus the One-eyed, under whom he served as an admiral. He wrote the *Achievements of Macedonia* in ten books, covering the history of the Argead kingdom down to Alexander, as well as the *Education of Alexander* and the *Deeds of Alexander* in five books. Unfortunately, these only survive in fragments quoted by other authors.

Aristobulus was an engineer on Alexander's staff and a close friend of the king. In his old age, beginning when he was 84, Aristobulus wrote his *Memoirs*, the chief events of which dealt with Alexander and the expedition. It was written specifically to refute Cleitarchus' mythologizing *History of Alexander*. Aristobulus wrote from memory and did not have access to the *Royal Journal*, but his general impressions were first-hand information.

Ptolemy I Soter, the son of Lagos, was possibly the illegitimate son of Philip II and thus Alexander's half-brother. In any event, Ptolemy was a boyhood friend and companion of Alexander, trained by Aristotle with Alexander and the other Royal Pages. He rose from Hetairos to Bodyguard (one of the *Somatophylakes*) for Alexander. Eventually he held both independent commands as a general under Alexander and as a taxiarch, one of Alexander's Field Marshals. He accompanied the entire expedition. After Alexander's death, Ptolemy was appointed as satrap of Egypt, and eventually became king, founding the XXX Dynasty of Egypt. He wrote a *History of Alexander* in his later years, after he had become Pharaoh himself, and had direct access to the *Royal Journal* as well as other original sources.

Finally, there were Nearchus, Alexander's Cretan admiral and friend, and Onesicritus. Though a Greek, Nearchus held Macedonian citizenship through the city of Amphipolis. He commanded the fleet returning with the wounded from India and left an account of his adventures in the Indian Ocean. Onesicritus of Astypalaia was Alexander's steersman and the second in command to Nearchus on the Indian voyage. He wrote a tribute to Alexander modeled after Xenophon's *Cyropaedia* but filled with tall tales and exaggeration.

Good or bad, none of these sources survive in anything but fragments quoted by others. There were other accounts as well, unknown to us. It was common for people who participated in the Napoleonic Wars, the European colonial experiences, and the World Wars (whether common soldiers, officers, or generals) to write up accounts of these events. So too did those who served with Alexander. We don't have those accounts, but the main literary sources we do have, to one degree or another, did have access to all of them.

Ancient Secondary Literary Sources

There are ancient works that mention Alexander incidentally, such as Strabo's *Geography* written in the first century B.C.E., or Pausanius' *Guide to Greece*, written in the second century C.E. Works of this sort provide some information, and like archaeology, can be a check on our main sources, but they are not systematic studies of history in general or Alexander in particular. There are five main literary sources from antiquity that do, however.

The earliest of these authors is Diodorus Siculus. He was a Greek from Agyrium on the island of

Sicily, born in the first century B.C.E., and a contemporary of Julius Caesar. He wrote the *Bibliotheca*, or the *Universal Library*. It was actually an attempt at writing world history, encompassing a history of both the Greek and Roman worlds in parallel events and development, written in some forty books. Only fifteen of these fully survive, and the rest are in fragments quoted by others. Among those surviving books is the fullest account of Greek events by a Greek author for the years from 359 to 301 B.C.E., the very years of Philip and Alexander. Diodorus is generally considered only as good as the sources he drew from, which sometimes were very good. For Philip, Diodorus used Ephorus, and for the events after Alexander, he relied on Hieronymus of Cardia, a cousin of Alexander's Greek secretary, Eumenes, who was later both a general under Antigonus and the royal archivist in Macedonia. Diodorus' accounts of Alexander's reign are a little more problematic. The suspicion is that a good deal of Cleitarchus' *History of Alexander* may have been slipped in here. Regardless, Diodorus is writing 300 years after the events.

Chronologically, the next source is Roman, Quintus Curtius Rufus, who was probably the Roman consul (chief magistrate) of the year 43 C.E. One of the imperial elite, Curtius was a man who rose in the imperial service to command the army and province of Upper Germany and died while the senatorial proconsul of the Province of Africa. Clearly, Curtius was a man of considerable military and political experience. He wrote a *History of Alexander the Great* in ten books, the first two of which are missing. Indeed, it was the Romans who gave Alexander the nickname of *Magnus*, "the Great," as the Greek epithet from Alexander's own time had been "Aniketos" (the Invincible).

Curtius' work is filled with speeches, largely made up by Curtius himself for his own moralizing purposes. He used sources as they suited his purpose. Curtius viewed matters from a Roman point of view, including reading Roman imperial court intrigue back into Alexander's time. Nevertheless, he used both Ptolemy and Cleitarchus, and possibly Marsyas of Pella, and as a result Curtius preserves a good deal of genuine Macedonian custom and practice not found elsewhere.

The next major literary source was Lucius Mestrius Plutarchus, who lived from about 50 to 110 C.E. Despite his Roman sounding name, Plutarch of Chaeronea was a Greek and a hereditary priest of Apollo at the Oracle of Delphi. That gave him access to one of the great libraries and archives of antiquity. Plutarch was best known as a philosopher, and his largest work was a series of essays usually lumped together as the *Moralia*. Well traveled, including Alexandria in Egypt and an extended time teaching in Rome, Plutarch was granted Roman citizenship and was probably the Procurator (or Governor) of Greece under the Emperor Trajan. He was another person of importance and experience.

Plutarch was best known both in antiquity and in modern times as the author of the *Parallel Lives*. This consisted of twenty-three pairs of matching lives, and nineteen comparisons of those lives, one in each pair being a Greek and one a Roman. Plutarch saw the achievements of these people as parallel to one another, hence the title. Among these are the lives of Caesar and Alexander. Indeed, it was in the opening part of the *Life of Alexander* that Plutarch laid out his purpose. He expressly stated that he was not writing history but that he meant to write of great men's characters, their virtues, and their vices. In doing that, small things, rather than great deeds, are often more revealing of that character. Plutarch was, in effect, the first psychological biographer, and meant the *Lives* to be a matter of instruction to the youth of his day and later. His influence historically, however, has been immense, and copies of Plutarch's *Lives* could be found in the private library of practically every educated household in Europe and America in the eighteenth, nineteenth, and twentieth centuries.

For Alexander, unfortunately, Plutarch relied heavily on Cleitarchus, so it is largely the romanticized (and popular) version that he preserves.

By far the best ancient account of Alexander's life is that of Lucius Flavius Arrianus, who came from the generation after Plutarch, and therefore almost 500 years after Alexander. Arrian was a student of the Stoic philosopher Epictetus, whose lectures Arrian preserved as the *Discourses*. Sponsored by the Emperor Hadrian, Arrian rose through the imperial service to become a Roman Consul (as Curtius had) and the imperial governor of the Province of Cappodocia in Asia Minor. When Arrian retired, he settled in Athens where he was elected Archon Eponymous (chief magistrate) for the year 145–146 C.E. He was, thus, the only known private person (not an emperor) to be both a Roman Consul and an Athenian Archon: a remarkable man.

Arrian wrote in Greek and saw himself as the new Xenophon: a student of philosophy, as Xenophon had been a student and preserver of Socrates; a serving general, as Xenophon had been in the Persian expedition which Xenophon himself chronicled in *The March of the 10,000* or the *Anabasis*; and as a historian, just as Xenophon had written a history of his times called the *Hellenika*. In writing of Alexander's campaigns, Arrian went so far as to call it the

Anabasis of Alexander, which Arrian wrote in seven books. His work on Alexander was easily and demonstrably the best researched. Arrian relied extensively on the *Royal Journal* and frequently cites Ptolemy, Aristobulus, and Nearchus in a work called the *Indika*, directly, as well as others. Arrian also wrote a history of the events immediately after Alexander's death, a period so complex that it took ten books to cover it. Arrian completed his imitation of Xenophon by writing both a *Treatise on Hunting Dogs* and a *Manual of Cavalry Tactics*, the latter of which was so good that both it and Xenophon's work were still being quoted extensively in the British Royal Army's *Manual of Equitation* in the twentieth century.

Finally, there is Marcus Junianus Justinus, who wrote sometime between the second and fourth centuries C.E. Justin's work was what is called an *epitome*, or a condensed version, of an earlier work, the *Philippic Histories of Pompeius Trogus*. The author of this earlier work, Trogus, was a Vocontian Gaul and the grandson of Julius Caesar's Celtic secretary. A Roman citizen, Trogus was commissioned by the Emperor Augustus to write a companion piece to Livy's *History of Rome*, which he did in forty-four books. We have only the chapter headings from this work, which Justin preserves, and Justin's *epitome* of the work itself.

Beginning with the ancient Near East and continuing down to Augustus' own time, the *epitome* of the *Philippic Histories* constitutes the only continuous source on Greek affairs that we have in any form. Books eight through forty covered Macedonia and its successor Hellenistic kingdoms, clearly the main part of the work. Justin terribly conflates Trogus' original work, tacking phrases from multiple sentences together in order to shorten things. In doing so, it frequently becomes difficult for us to discern how much altered by this process these are from the original meanings and events. Nevertheless, Trogus' *Philippic Histories* ranked as an equal alongside the works of the great Roman historians such as Sallust, Livy, and Tacitus in antiquity. Gems of information are hidden in Justin's abbreviation, but it must be used carefully.

All of these, taken with the artifacts, form the basis of source criticism and study for Alexander and his times. It is a picture that is continually being expanded by archaeology. Yet despite the fact that it amounts to a large body of material, it still leaves room for radically different interpretations of these events and personalities by modern scholars.

Modern Sources

The modern bibliography on Alexander is rich and extensive, comprising scholarly monographs, articles, and popular literature. For the purposes of this study, of necessity, this must be a highly selective list. Presuming that the reader is beginning the study of Macedonia and Alexander, this discussion is restricted to works in English. But one should note that the scholarship on Alexander in German, French, Italian, and (of course) Greek is immense, and the serious student at some point must come to grips with it.

The definitive study of Macedonia is the three-volume *A History of Macedonia* (Oxford, 1970–1988) by N.G.L. Hammond, G.T. Griffith, and F.W. Walbank. It is thorough, authoritative, and even magisterial, but designed for the serious student. Both Philip and Alexander are discussed at length. However, for someone just beginning, *In the Shadow of Olympus: the Emergence of Macedon* (Princeton, 1990) by E.N. Borza is highly recommended. Extremely well written, this work covers developments through Philip II and is especially good in dealing with the geography, environment, and material culture of Macedonia. Also, for those interested in gender studies, E.D. Carney's *Women and Monarchy in Macedonia* (Norman, OK, 2000) is a welcome addition.

For Philip II in particular, the sections written by Guy Griffith in the second volume of *A History of Macedonia* are among the best things ever written on Philip. The standard scholarly biography is still George Cawkwell's *Philip of Macedon* (London, 1978) though it is somewhat dated. One should also look at N.G.L. Hammond's *Philip of Macedon* (Baltimore, 1994) which is the culmination of a career's worth of study on Macedonia and Philip. Alfred S. Bradford's *Philip II of Macedon: A Life from the Ancient Sources* (Westport, CT, 1992) is a useful compendium of the ancient material. A handy collection of original essays from the best scholars in the field can be found in *Philip of Macedon* (Athens, 1980), edited by M.B. Hatzopuoulos and L.D. Loukopoulos. Finally, on Philip and his role in building a Macedonian state, see J.R. Ellis' *Philip II and Macedonian Imperialism* (London, 1976).

For a general introduction to Alexander studies, a good place to start is with *Alexander the Great: Ancient and Modern Perspectives* (Lexington, 1995), edited by Joseph Roisman. This has selections from ancient sources and modern scholars arranged topically. A more extensive look at sources (also arranged topically by problem) is *Alexander the Great: Historical Sources in Translation* (Oxford, 2004), translated and edited by Waldemar Heckel and J.C. Yardley. Finally, *Brill's Companion to Alexander the Great* (Leiden, 2003), edited by Joseph Roisman, is extensive and extremely useful.

In terms of biographies of Alexander, the range is huge. The most significant and serious study of recent years has been the ongoing works of A.B. Bosworth. *Conquest and Empire: the Reign of Alexander the Great* (Cambridge, 1988) and *Alexander and the East: The Tragedy of Triumph* (Oxford, 1998) have dominated the field. Though covering the narrative fairly quickly, Bosworth has concentrated on interpretative essays of Alexander. Accompanying them have been source studies such as *From Arrian to Alexander: Studies in Historical Interpretation* (Oxford 1988) and *A Historical Commentary on Arrian's History of Alexander*, vol. I (Oxford, 1980) and vol. II (Oxford, 1995), with more to follow. No serious student of Alexander can ignore these, though they are not easily accessible to the beginner and frequently express strong views of Alexander that are not mainstream and so must be read with caution.

By far the most readable single-volume modern biography of Alexander is Peter Green's *Alexander of Macedon, 356–323 B.C. An Historical Biography* (Berkeley, 1991). Literate and well written, Green covers Alexander's life with a strong, vibrant, and highly informed narrative style. Other works include Ulrich Wilcken's *Alexander the Great* (New York, reprint in 1977), a translation based on a much earlier edition.

Wilcken's book is useful but dated and somewhat stilted in style. Sir William Woodthorpe Tarn's *Alexander the Great* 2 vols. (Cambridge, 1948) is still available in reprint. This is the study of one of the great Alexander scholars. The first volume covers the narrative biography and the second volume deals with the sources. Though dated, and like Bosworth in expressing some strong views of Alexander (although at the other end of the interpretive spectrum), Tarn still has some interesting things to say. Finally, N.G.L. Hammond's *Alexander the Great: King, Commander and Statesman* 2nd ed. (Bristol, 1989) and *The Genius of Alexander the Great* (Chapel Hill, 1997), are a match to his *Philip of Macedon*, the result of a lifetime of study.

A number of specialty studies on Alexander are worth noting. Donald W. Engels' *Alexander the Great and the Logistics of the Macedonian Army* (Berkeley, 1978) is a standard. Equally, *The Cities of Alexander the Great* (Oxford, 1996) by P.M. Fraser and R A. Billows' *Kings and Colonists: Aspects of Macedonian Imperialism* (Leiden, 1995) deal extensively with the impact of Alexander's policies. James R. Ashley's *The Macedonian Empire: The Era of Warfare Under Philip II and Alexander the Great, 359–323 B.C.* (Jefferson, NC & London, 1998) does a solid job with the military history aspects of the period. Most useful in keeping the cast of characters straight is Waldemar Heckel's *The Marshals of Alexander's Empire* (London, 1992).

As Alexander's impact in Asia is frequently not as appreciated as his accomplishments in the West, two works by Frank L. Holt are worth noting. The first is *Alexander the Great and Bactria: the Formation of a Greek Frontier in Central Asia* (Leiden, 1989) which is essential, and the followup to W.W. Tarn's standard *The Greeks in Bactria and India* (Cambridge, 1951) and *Thundering Zeus: the Making of Hellenistic Bactria* (Berkeley, 1999). Most recently Holt has published *Alexander the Great and the Mystery of the Elephant Medallions* (Berkeley, 2003) which is an excellent example of how to use numismatic evidence (coins) in the historical narrative, and it is a good read beyond that.

Finally, in terms of the immediate legacy of Alexander, there is Peter Green's magisterial *Alexander to Actium: the Historical Evolution of the Hellenistic Age* (Berkeley, 1990). Typically well written, Green ranges across the full spectrum of political, social, and cultural topics in describing the world that came after Alexander. Equally useful, but perhaps not with the same sweep, is Frank W. Walbank's *The Hellenistic World*, Revised Ed. (Cambridge, MA., 1990).

There are, of course, many more than this and thousands more in article literature and popular literature. Scholarly symposia are held on Alexander as a special topic almost annually. Many will have favorites not mentioned above. But the intention here, as with this biography, is to provide a beginning to the study of Alexander the Great.

Glossary

Aegae: The ancient capitol of the Argead Kingdom of Macedonia, which was usually referred to as the "hearth of the kingdom" and the site for the royal tombs. It was located in what is the modern site of Vergina.

Agema: Refers to the lead regiment of the Household Gaurds or the lead squadron of the Companion Cavalry in the Macedonian army, units personally led by the King.

Agrianians: Hill tribe from Illyria, and formidable light troops. As mercenaries, they formed a unit of javelin men, which were among Alexander's favorites and frequently fought alongside the Companion Cavalry.

Amyntas III: The father of Philip II and the grandfather of Alexander the Great

Andropodysmos: A Greek term that means a "breaking" or "shattering" of the people. It refers to the punishment of a city or state that involves killing the adult male population, selling the women and children into slavery and razing the settlement to the ground.

Antipater: Philip II's most trusted general, who frequently served as Regent in Macedonia in the king's absence. In Alexander's reign he was the "General for Europe" and ruled the kingdom all during Alexander's campaigns in Asia.

Arete: Greek term that is usually translated as "excellence" but really means the "capacity for excellence" or "prowess." It is the Homeric Ideal to which all Heroes aspire and a driving principle in Alexander's character.

Argead: Name usually given to Alexander's family as the ruling dynasty of Macedonia. An alternative name for the family occasionally used is "Temenid" because they traced their descent from Herakles and it was his family's name.

Babylon: Ancient city in Mesopotamia, which was a royal Persian residence and the capitol of a satrapy. It will also serve as the chief administrative center for Alexander's civil government in Asia.

Bactria: Satrapy in eastern Iran in part of what is modern Afghanistan.

Basileus: Greek term meaning "king" or "chief" and the official title of the King of Macedonia. In Macedonia, the army assembly chose the king from among the adult male members of the Argead Royal House.

Basilikoi Paides: Greek term meaning the "royal boys" that refers to the Royal Pages. These were noble youths, included the princes of the Argead House, who served as squires and attendants while they were trained to arms and to take their place in the Macedonian army.

Bardyllis: Illyrian chieftain who overran the upper Macedonian tribal districts and killed Perdikkas III

(Philip II's brother and Alexander the Great's uncle). This event brought Philip to the throne, and Bardyllis defeat was Philip's first great victory in battle.

Bessus: Iranian satrap of Bactria, who killed Darius III and assumed the title of Great King. He constituted a major challenge to Alexander's authority after the defeat of Darius and initiated a bitter guerilla war in Afghanistan.

Callisthenes: Nephew of the philosopher Aristotle. He accompanied Alexander's expedition as the chief historian and propagandist. He later also tutored the Royal Pages when they were brought out to join the expedition.

Cardaces: Refers to Iranian infantry, sometimes called the "cadets" because the Corps of 10,000 Immortals that formed the Persian Household Guard was drawn from them.

Cassander: Son of Antipater, who did not accompany the expedition. He was later sent as an envoy of Antipater to Alexander in Babylon. Cassander ultimately became the successor to Alexander as King of Macedonia.

Chalcidic League: An alliance of some 20 Greek poleis on the Chalcidic Peninsula (just east of Macedonia). With its capitol at Olynthus, this was a major challenge to Macedonia. Philip II broke it up and incorporated the lands directly into the Macedonian state.

Chiliarch: Greek term literally meaning the "commander of a thousand" or a regiment (a chiliarchy). In the Persian context, as a title, it referred to the commander of the lead regiment of the Corps of 10,000 Immortals, and the Great King's personal bodyguards. But in practical terms this person was the "prime minister" of the Persian Empire.

Coenus: Macedonian noble and general under Alexander. Following Parmenio's murder, Coenus became the chief Macedonian spokesman in the army and Alexander's military second in command.

Craterus: Macedonian noble and general under Alexander. He took Coenus' place following his death in India.

Diadochoi: Greek term meaning the "Successors" that refers to the immediate successors of Alexander the Great, those who served with or were alive during Alexander's reign.

Dion: Religious site in Macedonia, at the foot of Mt. Olympus. The festival in honor of Zeus and the Nine Muses was held here.

Delphic Amphictyony: Religious League made up of all Greek states that administered the Oracle of Apollo at Delphi in Central Greece. It was the only permanent Panhellenic forum, and from 346 on the majority of votes were controlled first by Philip and then by Alexander.

Ecbatana: Modern Hamadan in the Zagros Mountains east of Mesopotamia, this was one of the Persian royal residences, the Summer Palace, and capitol of the satrapy of Media. It was one of the major staging points for Alexander's campaigns in eastern Asia.

Emathia: Also known as Bottiaia, this was one of the original tribal areas of the Argead monarchy and part of the Macedonia heartland. The chief city was Pella, the Macedonian administrative capitol.

Ephemerides: The "Day Book" or Royal Journal kept by Alexander's chief secretary, Eumenes of Cardia. All official orders, reports and accounts were kept in it.

Epirus: Area west of Macedonia (around modern Ioannina) which formed a separate league of tribes related to the Macedonians. The king of the tribe of the Molossi was the head of the League. Alexander's mother, Olympias, was a princess of this royal house.

Gedrosian Desert: The modern Makran Desert in southern Iran, this was the site of Alexander's horrifying march back from India.

Hegemon: A Greek term meaning "Leader" frequently applied to the head of an alliance system, whether a state like Sparta or Athens, of an individual, and hence the term "hegemony." It was the term applied to both Philip and later Alexander as the commander of the League of Corinth's military forces: the "Captain General of Greece."

Hetairoi: Greek term meaning "companion." This was applied as a social group to the nobles of Macedonian, and specifically to the Companion Cavalry that formed the elite mounted force of the Macedonia army.

Hipparch: A Greek term meaning the "commander of horsemen." Specifically, it was usually applied to the commander of a cavalry squadron (or hipparchy) 300 men.

Homonoia: A Greek term meaning "equality." It was a frequent component of treaty relations implying the legal status of the signatories, but also refers to the principle of equality and therefore harmony (in theory).

Hoplite: Greek term applied to a heavy infantryman, one who carried a *hoplon* or large round shield.

Hypaspists: A Greek term meaning the "long shields." This was the nickname of the three regiments (chiliarchies) that formed the Macedonian Guards Brigade. It was sometimes called the Pezetairoi or "Foot Companions" and formed the elite infantry unit of the Macedonian army.

Illyria: Large tribal are in the Balkans Northwest and North of Macedonia in what is now Albania, Kosovo, Serbia Montenegro, and the former Yugoslavian Republic of Macedonia. Illyrians spoke a dialect Indo-European akin to Greek and posed one of the chief external threats to the Macedonian Kingdom.

Isegoria: In effect the right of petition and free speech in Macedonia. This was a right taken seriously by both monarch and people and which distinguished the Macedonians in Greek eyes from the other subjects of kings whom the Greeks regarded as natural slaves.

Isocrates: Noted Athenian orator who saw the influence of Persian gold on Greek politics and called for Greeks to put aside their squabbles to unite in a common war against Persia. He wrote to all of the important political figures of his times urging this enterprise, but it was Philip II who took up the challenge and ultimately passed it on to Alexander.

Kleitos the Black: Macedonian noble who commanded the Agema (the King's Own) squadron of the Companion Cavalry.

Koine Eirene: Greek for "Common Peace," this was a standard clause of peace treaties in the Fourth Century B.C.E. that ensured the cessation of hostilities. It was also a fundamental part of the establishment of the League of Corinth by Philip II.

Koinonia: Greek term meaning to make a "Common Cause" and later to make a common community. It was one of the points urged by Alexander at the Feast at Opis.

Koinon: Greek term meaning "Common Thing" and the equivalent of the Latin term *Res Publica* (Republic). It generally meant a federal league, such as the Thessalian League, referring to a permanent political structure.

Koine: A Greek term usually applied to the common Greek dialect based on Attic Greek which emerged throughout the Greek world and Near East after Alexander's death.

League of Corinth: The alliance system put together by Philip II following the Battle of Chaeronea. It provided for a common peace, means of resolving disputes, and a collective security arrangement. Philip was to be Hegemon to command the Greek. It was the League which declared war on Persia. On Philip's death, Alexander inherited both the Hegemony and the war.

Lynkestis: This was an important highland tribal district in Macedonia, whose ruling family was particularly influential at court.

Memnon of Rhodes: The commander of the mercenary Greek forces in the Persian Empire, which was a position previously held by his brother Mentor. Memnon had been an exile in Macedonia and knew its political weaknesses. He was the most serious challenge to Alexander's expedition.

Memphis: The ancient capitol of united Egypt and the center of Persian administration in the satrapy of Egypt.

Mieza: Near modern Naoussa in Macedonia, this was the site where Aristotle tutored Alexander and the other Royal Pages.

Nicanor: This was a son of Parmenio, and friend of Alexander. He commanded the Hypapspists (Guards Brigade), the elite infantry unit of the Macedonian army until his death on campaign in 331.

Oasis of Siwah: This was the site of the Oracle of Zeus Ammon in the Libyan Desert, which was visited by Alexander.

Olympias: Alexander's mother, Olympias was an Epirote princess.

Oxyartes: An Iranian chieftain from Sogdiana and one of the leaders of the guerilla resistance to Alexander. Alexander eventually brought peace by marrying his daughter (Roxane) and incorporating the Sogdians directly into the Macedonian forces.

Paeonia: A tribal district just North of Macedonia.

Parmenio: He was one of Philip's most trusted generals, frequently given independent commands. During the expedition, he was the senior member of Alexander's staff and his second in command until Alexander ordered his death in 330.

Pasagardae: This was the original capitol of the Persian Empire under Cyrus, and the site of his tomb.

Pella: The administrative and economic capitol of the Macedonian kingdom.

Pelta: A Greek term referring to a small round target shield (roughly 18" in diameter) carried by light armed troops (who were called *peltasts* to distinguish them from hoplites).

Persepolis: This was the capitol of the Persian Empire, built by Darius the Great. It held the ceremonial palace and was the main seat of administration.

Phalanx: The Greek term for a formation of heavy infantry-men (hoplites), who were in turn called *phalangites*. Under Philip and Alexander formation could vary in length, depending on the numbers present and the type of front needed. It was normally 8 ranks deep, but could be and was frequently deepened or formed into two separate battle lines.

Philip II: He was Alexander's father and the architect of the Macedonian army, the Macedonian state and the League of Corinth, all of which were essential to Alexander.

Philotas: A friend of Alexander's and Parmenio's eldest son, he commanded the Companion Cavalry until he was executed by Alexander in 330.

Pieria: This was one of the original tribal districts in the heartland of Macedonia and the site of the traditional capitol, Aegae.

Polis: The Greek term usually translated as "city-state," its real meaning is more akin to "community."

Pothos: The Greek term for an "undeniable urge," many of which seemed to seize Alexander on his long journey to justifying far away places.

Proskynesis: The Greek term for the Persian court practice of abasing yourself in the presence of the Great King by throwing yourself flat on the floor in front of the imperial person.

Ptolemy: He was known as the son of Lagos (both as the normal patronymic and to distinguish him from other Ptolemies at court as this was a popular Macedonian name). A boyhood friend of Alexander, he rose from Hetairos, to Somatophylax (Bodyguard), to taxiarch (brigadier) and independent commander. He eventually became the king of Egypt after Alexander's death and founded the XXX Dynasty.

Satrap: This was the term for the governor of a Persian imperial province (*satrapy*). The satrap held full civil, military, and economic authority within his province. Alexander altered this in his reorganization, splitting the military authority out of the office and centralizing the economic functions, which left the satrap as civil governor only.

Sogdiana: This was an eastern Persian satrapy next to Bactria in part of what is now mostly modern Afghanistan.

Somatophylakes: A Greek term which literally means "guardians of the sleep," these were technically Alexander's bodyguards. Drawn from among the Hetairoi, these consisted of eight men specially chosen by Alexander for their loyalty and were positions of considerable status at court.

Susa: This was a city which controlled the main pass through the Zagros Mts. East of Mesopotamia. It was a royal residence and mint and the nexus for the imperial roads which crossed the East/West communications of the Persian Empire.

Symposium: This is a Greek term referring to a "feast" and as a formal event an important part of Macedonian court ritual.

Synderion: This is the Greek term meaning a "council" and was the name given to the governing body in the League of Corinth.

Tagos: This was the Greek term applied to the war commander of the Thessalian League, a position occupied by both Philip II and later Alexander.

Talent: This is the Greek term applied to a unit of weight, in the Attic standard the equivalent of 25.86 kilograms. In terms of silver, it was the standard measure of an economy.

Taxiarch: This is the Greek term for the commander of a taxsis, or brigade. In Macedonian terms this unit amounted to 1500 heavy infantrymen (hoplites) and there were ten such units in the Macedonian army.

Thrace: This was an extreme area covering almost all of the eastern Balkan Peninsula. It contained numerous tribes who spoke an Indo-European dialect vaguely related to (but not) Greek. This region was the main target of Philip II's plans for expanding the Macedonian state.

Zoroastrianism: The religion of Iranians and the official religion of the Acheamenid Dynasty of Persia from Darius the Great onwards.

Index